UNLOCK YOUR IMAGINATION

Illustrated by Peter Judson

CONTENTS

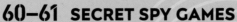

In **Unlock Your Imagination**, you can choose from **256 amazing activities** that are guaranteed to keep you entertained. From making your own obstacle course and pranking your friends, to inventing your own board game and making slime, there's **something for everyone**.

Clear step-by-step instructions guide you through the activities.

Checklists tell you everything you need before you start a project.

Each activity is numbered so you can keep track of how many you've completed.

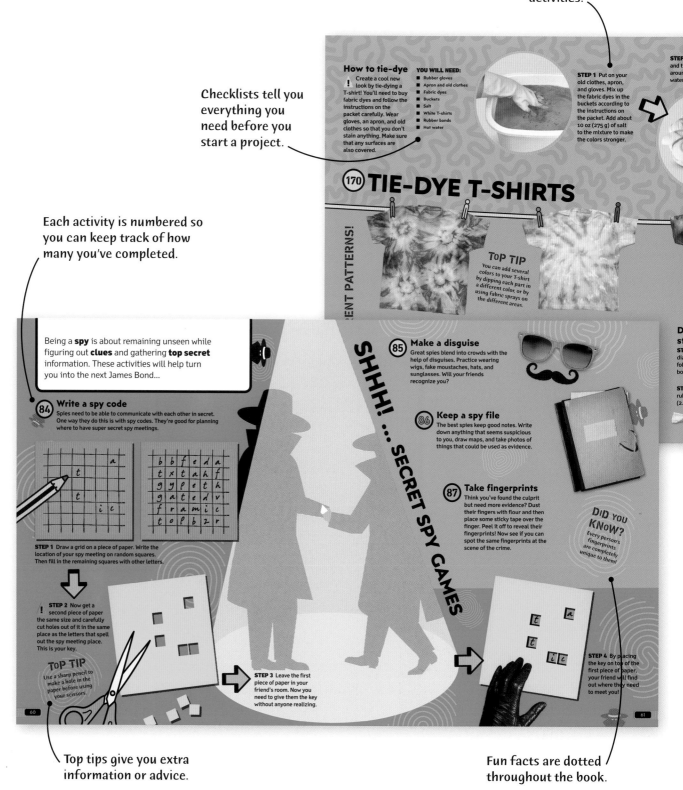

How to tie-dye

Create a cool new look by tie-dying a T-shirt! You'll need to buy fabric dyes and follow the instructions on the packet carefully. Wear gloves, an apron, and old clothes so that you don't stain anything. Make sure that any surfaces are also covered.

YOU WILL NEED:
- Rubber gloves
- Apron and old clothes
- Fabric dyes
- Buckets
- Salt
- White T-shirts
- Rubber bands
- Hot water

STEP 1 Put on your old clothes, apron, and gloves. Mix up the fabric dyes in the buckets according to the instructions on the packet. Add about 10 oz (275 g) of salt to the mixture to make the colors stronger.

STEP and tie around water

(170) **TIE-DYE T-SHIRTS**

TOP TIP
You can add several colors to your T-shirt by dipping each part in a different color, or by using fabric sprays on the different areas.

Being a **spy** is about remaining unseen while figuring out **clues** and gathering **top secret** information. These activities will help turn you into the next James Bond...

(84) **Write a spy code**
Spies need to be able to communicate with each other in secret. One way they do this is with spy codes. They're good for planning where to have super secret spy meetings.

STEP 1 Draw a grid on a piece of paper. Write the location of your spy meeting on random squares. Then fill in the remaining squares with other letters.

STEP 2 Now get a second piece of paper the same size and carefully cut holes out of it in the same place as the letters that spell out the spy meeting place. This is your key.

TOP TIP
Use a sharp pencil to make a hole in the paper before using your scissors.

STEP 3 Leave the first piece of paper in your friend's room. Now you need to give them the key without anyone realizing.

(85) **Make a disguise**
Great spies blend into crowds with the help of disguises. Practice wearing wigs, fake moustaches, hats, and sunglasses. Will your friends recognize you?

(86) **Keep a spy file**
The best spies keep good notes. Write down anything that seems suspicious to you, draw maps, and take photos of things that could be used as evidence.

(87) **Take fingerprints**
Think you've found the culprit but need more evidence? Dust their fingers with flour and then place some sticky tape over the finger. Peel it off to reveal their fingerprints! Now see if you can spot the same fingerprints at the scene of the crime.

DID YOU KNOW?
Every person's fingerprints are completely unique to them!

SHHHH! ....SECRET SPY GAMES

STEP 4 By placing the key on top of the first piece of paper, your friend will find out where they need to meet you!

Top tips give you extra information or advice.

Fun facts are dotted throughout the book.

Want to get your imagination working in overdrive? These pages will give you lots of ideas about how you can use everyday items, such as paper cups and sticks, in fun new ways.

247 Fire-breather
⚠ Fix seven cups together to make your very own dragon. Poke small holes in the side of each cup with a pencil, then use paper fasteners to hold them together. Stick on googly eyes, draw the mouth and nose with a marker, and use white paper for the teeth. For a final flourish, add pipe cleaners to the nose.

248 Flower-grower
Fill your cup with soil and plant seeds. Add a sprinkle of water, and watch your flowers grow. Make sure there is a hole in the bottom so excess water can escape.

249 Noise-maker
Tape the open ends of two cups together, with some dried beans or pieces of pasta inside. Add streamers for style. You've made your very own maraca!

250 Friend-caller
Poke a hole in the bottom of two cups. Get a long piece of string, and thread one end through each cup, finishing in a knot. When you pull the string taut and talk into one cup, your friend will hear you through the other.

SQUAWK!

251 Nose-changer
Draw the noses of animals on cups and gather your friends. Hold the cups in front of your faces and witness the transformation!

THINGS TO DO WITH... A PAPER CUP!

253 Headband-decorator
⚠ Cut triangles out of a cup's rim, glue pompoms to the top, and attach the cup to a headband to make a crown fit for royalty.

254 Sea-dweller
With a bit of paint and a pair of scissors, you can turn a paper cup into an eight-legged pet! Curl up the paper tentacles using a pencil, and give your octopus eyes and a smile for extra fun.

255 Pom-pom-popper
⚠ Cut off the bottom of a cup, and cut off the top of a balloon. Tie the end of the balloon in a knot, then wrap it around the cup. Add mini pom-poms to the cup, pull the knot, and—pop! Always aim it away from you and other people.

256 Cup-flipper
Place a cup on the edge of a table. Use one finger to push up against the cup's bottom to make it flip. Once you've got it, see how many you can land upside-down in a row, or in a minute.
The cup should flip all the way over in midair.

153

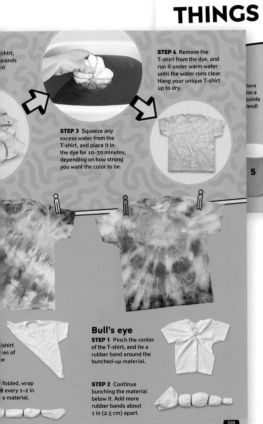

STEP 4 Remove the T-shirt from the dye, and run it under warm water until the water runs clear. Hang your unique T-shirt up to dry.

STEP 3 Squeeze any excess water from the T-shirt, and place it in the dye for 10–30 minutes, depending on how strong you want the color to be.

...shirt, ...ands ...t

...lace ...ss a ...points ...end!

5

Bull's eye
STEP 1 Pinch the center of the T-shirt, and tie a rubber band around the bunched-up material.

STEP 2 Continue bunching the material below it. Add more rubber bands about 1 in (2.5 cm) apart.

...shirt, ...es of ...e

...folded, wrap ...t every 1–2 in ...e material.

109

Important note to parents
The activities in this book may require adult help and supervision, depending on your child's age and ability. Always ensure that your child uses tools that are appropriate to their age, and offer help and supervision as necessary to keep them safe. The Publisher cannot accept any liability for injury, loss, or damage to any property or user following suggestions in this book.

Unlock your imagination!
When you see the padlock, it means it's time to get creative and come up with your own ideas. Don't be held back by the activities in this book—the sky's the limit!

Warning symbol
When you see the warning symbol on an activity, it means you will need an adult to help or supervise you. Keep an eye out for these symbols throughout the book!

Take particular care when:
- An activity requires the use of sharp objects, such as scissors, knives, pins, or wire.
- An activity involves heat.
- An activity may cause staining, such as when you're making slime.
- An activity can't be done in the safety of your home. It's important to always be aware of your surroundings.
- An activity involves going out at night or playing in the dark.

① CAPTURE THE FLAG

To win this game, you'll need both **speed** and **strategy**. Your objective: to steal the other team's flag and bring it back to your side **without getting tagged**. Gather two teams of at least four players each, choose a big outdoor space to play in, and let the game begin!

Defenders

One strategy is to split your team into two groups: attackers and defenders. The defenders stay on their team's side and try to tag any invaders from the other side.

If you make it to the other side without being seen, hide until you have a chance to snatch the flag.

"Guarding" your flag, or standing too close to it, is against the rules.

Flag

The flag is the name of the game—literally! Protect it at all costs. If the other team captures it and brings it back to their side without being tagged, it's game over.

Always keep an eye out for any attackers who may have crossed the line unnoticed.

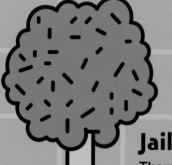

Jail

There are two "jails," one on each side. When players are caught and tagged, they have to go to jail and wait there until they are freed.

MAKE IT TOUGHER

Finding it a little too easy? You can raise the stakes...

Allow each team to partially hide their flag so that only a bit of it is showing.

⚠ Get an adult's permission to play at night with only head lamps or flashlights for light.

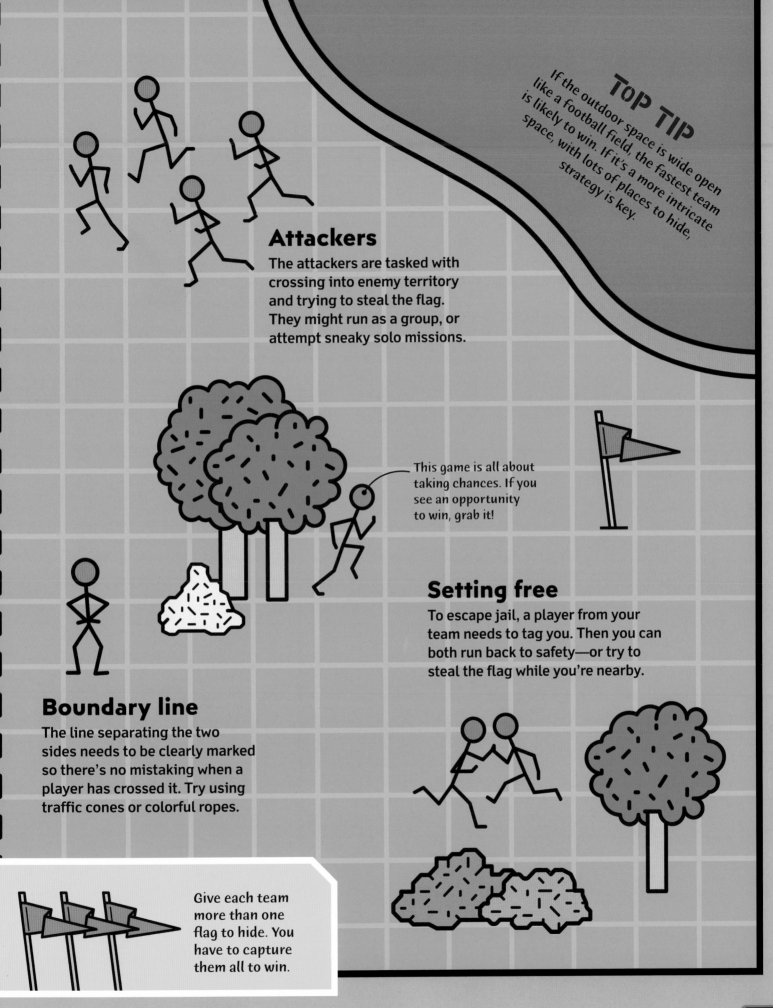

TOP TIP

If the outdoor space is wide open like a football field, the fastest team is likely to win. If it's a more intricate space, with lots of places to hide, strategy is key.

Attackers

The attackers are tasked with crossing into enemy territory and trying to steal the flag. They might run as a group, or attempt sneaky solo missions.

This game is all about taking chances. If you see an opportunity to win, grab it!

Setting free

To escape jail, a player from your team needs to tag you. Then you can both run back to safety—or try to steal the flag while you're nearby.

Boundary line

The line separating the two sides needs to be clearly marked so there's no mistaking when a player has crossed it. Try using traffic cones or colorful ropes.

Give each team more than one flag to hide. You have to capture them all to win.

TAG GAMES

Most people know how to play tag. Whoever is "**it**" runs around trying to **catch everyone else**. All you need to play the game is an open space and a group of people. Here are five ways to **change up** this classic game.

② **Zombie tag**

Choose one person in your group to be a groaning zombie. The humans have to run away from the zombie and try not to be touched—when a human is touched by a zombie, they become one. The winner of the game is the last human that has not been turned into a zombie.

⑤ **Amoeba tag**

In this game, two people are "it." They have to hold hands and try to surround other players, like an amoeba. Anyone they catch has to hold hands as well, making the chain longer. When the chain is four people long, "it" can stay together or split into two pairs of two. They can link back together later if they want. Amoeba tag is played until there is nobody left to catch.

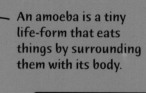

An amoeba is a tiny life-form that eats things by surrounding them with its body.

④ **Freeze tag**

Choose one person to be "it." "It" chases the other players around. If "it" touches someone, that person has to freeze. A frozen player is not allowed to move until another player touches them to free them. Once freed the frozen player can rejoin the game. "It" wins the game when all the players have been frozen.

You'll need a scarf for the tail of the dragon.

Red rover

For this game, you need at least six people, split into two teams. The teams start by linking their arms together to make two chains facing each other.

Then one team calls a player from the other side, saying, "Red rover, red rover, send [name] on over!" The person named must run out of their line and try to break through the other team's chain. If they can't break through, they join the other team.

If the person does break through, they can capture one of the two players whose link they broke, and take that player back with them to their original team.

The teams take turns calling red rover. The game ends when all of the players are on one side.

⑥ **Dragon tag**

Make at least two teams of four people. Each team forms a chain, with players holding the waist of the person in front of them. The person at the front of the chain is the head of the dragon, and the person at the back is the tail. Hang a scarf from the back pocket of the tail person. The aim is to have the head of a dragon grab the scarf off the other dragons while everyone stays linked. If a dragon breaks apart, the players cannot chase other dragons until their dragon is back together. When a team loses their scarf, they are out. The last team remaining wins!

TOP TIP

If you need a break, call a "time out"— everyone stays where they are and can rest until you're all ready to play again.

⑦ WRITE A STORY

Do you want to be the next **J. K. Rowling**? Let your creative ideas loose on the **page** and you might just be. So pick up a **pen** and get lost in your very own world of **imagination**.

Always make sure that the setting suits the story you're writing.

Decide on a genre

It might be helpful to select a genre for your story before you start writing it. This is the type of story you want to tell. Will it be fantasy, sci-fi, mystery, or adventure? These are just a few suggestions to get you started, but there are plenty more to choose from!

Fantasy

Science fiction

MYSTERY

Adventure

Choose a setting

Next you need to choose where your story will take place. How about a graveyard for a ghost story, a deserted island for an adventure, or a castle for a fairy tale? Remember, you don't always have to stick to just one.

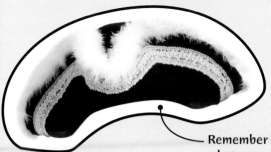

Remember to describe what your characters are wearing. This will make it easier for your readers to imagine them.

Perfect the plot

You've selected the genre, setting, and characters. Now all that's left to do is decide what's going to take place in the rest of your story.

- Sometimes the hardest part about writing a story is starting it. Once you've got your first few lines, the rest should follow.

- If you're stuck for ideas, read some pages from your favorite book. Figure out what you love about that story and how you can write something similar.

- Some of the best stories include an unexpected twist. Add one at the end to surprise your readers.

- Think of a title that perfectly sums up your story. Try to make it engaging so that people want to read it.

Select the characters

Every story needs characters. Decide how many you want and who the main character or characters are going to be. You might want to base them on people you know.

Maybe one of your characters could wear a mask to hide their identity.

Read it aloud to friends and family

Once you've put pen to paper, ask your friends and family to listen to your story. They might have some suggestions to help make it even better or a great idea for the sequel!

PUT ON A PLAY!

Let's put on a **performance**! To create your own **play** you'll need some friends and a lot of **imagination**. Here are some ideas to help you write and perform your own play.

8 Write a script

A script tells you what will happen in a play, as well as what the different characters say. What sort of script will you write?

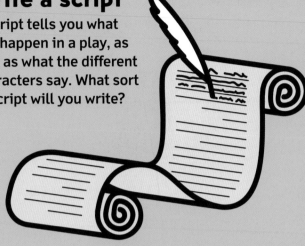

9 Make some props

! Every play needs costumes and props (objects) to make it realistic. You could buy props or get creative and make your own, such as this crown and sword.

Crown

If your play has any kings or queens in it, they will need crowns to make them look the part.

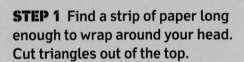

STEP 1 Find a strip of paper long enough to wrap around your head. Cut triangles out of the top.

STEP 2 Color your crown, then draw some jewels and stick them on. Tape the ends together to finish.

Sword

Pretend fighting will look much more realistic if your characters have swords!

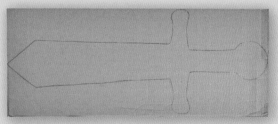

STEP 1 Draw a sword shape onto cardboard, then cut it out.

STEP 2 Decorate with color and tinfoil.

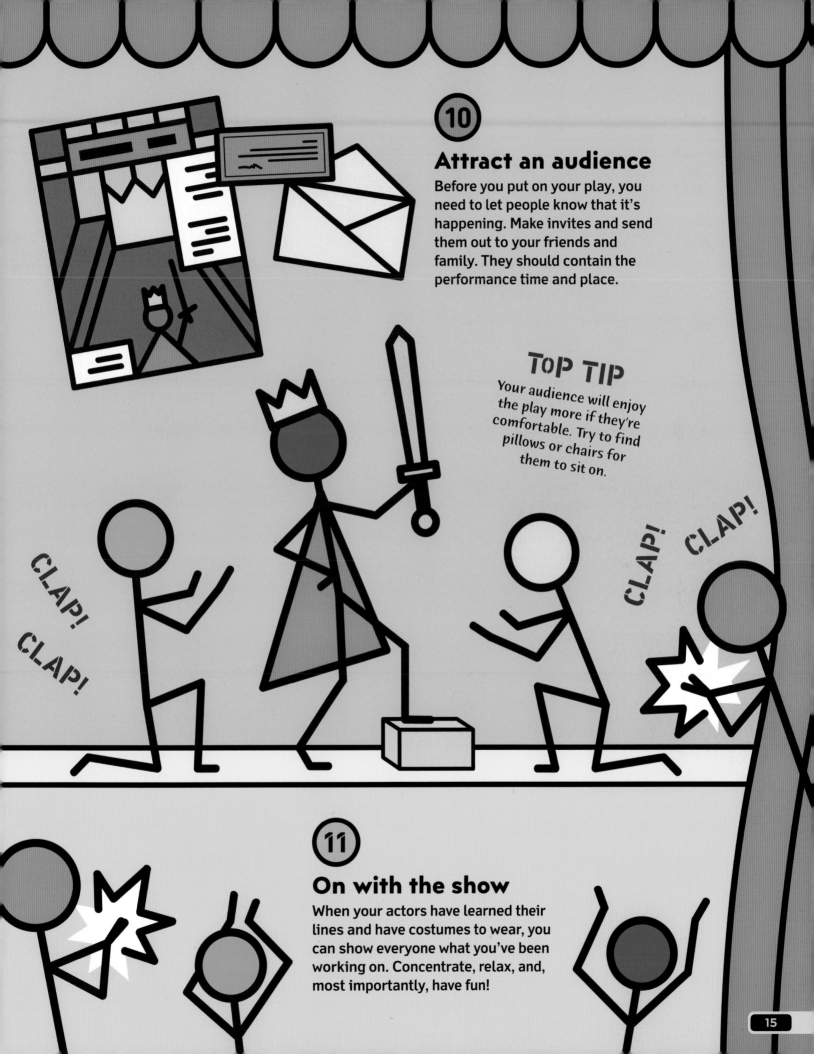

10 Attract an audience

Before you put on your play, you need to let people know that it's happening. Make invites and send them out to your friends and family. They should contain the performance time and place.

TOP TIP

Your audience will enjoy the play more if they're comfortable. Try to find pillows or chairs for them to sit on.

CLAP!
CLAP!
CLAP!

CLAP!
CLAP!

11 On with the show

When your actors have learned their lines and have costumes to wear, you can show everyone what you've been working on. Concentrate, relax, and, most importantly, have fun!

DANCE PARTY

Quiet day? Try making things more exciting with your own **dance party**! You'll need **music** and maybe a friend or two to dance with. You could even plan a crazy **dance routine**. Here are some simple moves to get you started.

⑬ Lawn mower

This dance comes in four steps. First, start the imaginary mower by pulling from low down to up high—as if you were starting an engine. Second, drive the mower along, with your hands out in front of you. Third, wipe away the sweat from your forehead with one hand and then the other. Finally, empty the grass from the mower by throwing it over your shoulder.

⑫ Arm wave

This move will make it look like a wave of energy is passing along your arms. Start with your arms out on each side of you, making a "T" shape. Bend your wrist down, then your elbow. Lift your elbow back up, then lift your shoulder. Bring your shoulder back down, and lift your other shoulder up. Then repeat the moves down your other arm. To make the wave look good, you need to move smoothly from one step to the next.

Ancient Egyptians wrote using symbols called hieroglyphs.

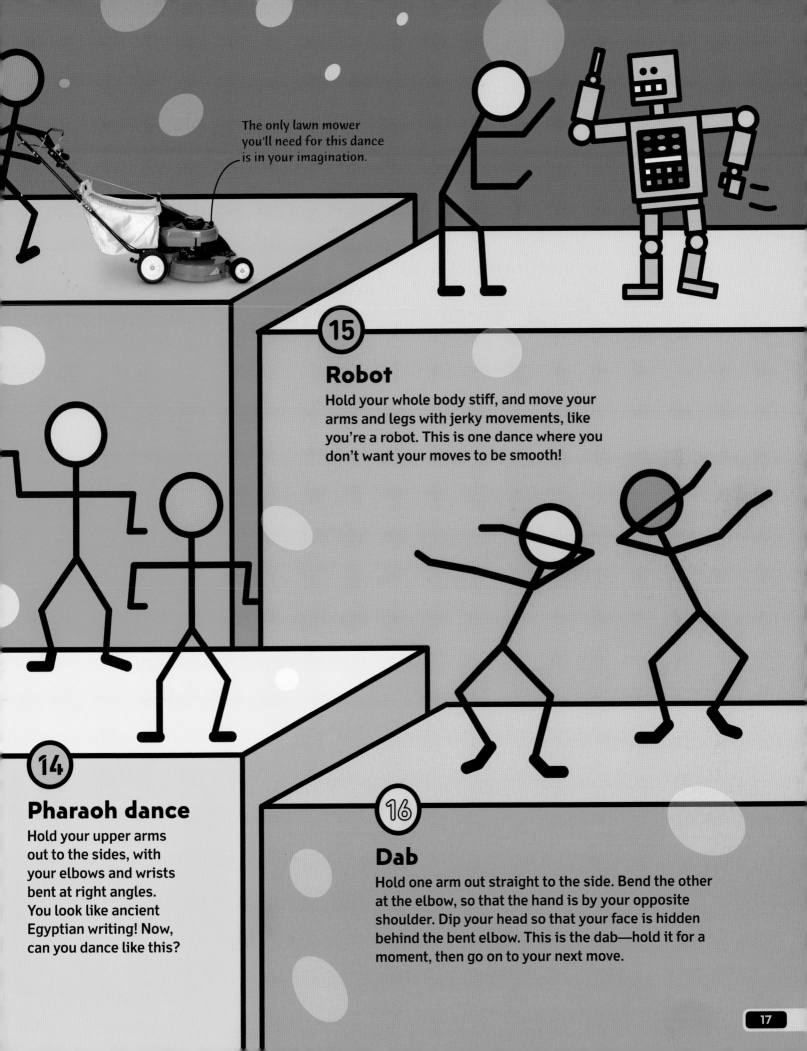

The only lawn mower you'll need for this dance is in your imagination.

15

Robot

Hold your whole body stiff, and move your arms and legs with jerky movements, like you're a robot. This is one dance where you don't want your moves to be smooth!

14

Pharaoh dance

Hold your upper arms out to the sides, with your elbows and wrists bent at right angles. You look like ancient Egyptian writing! Now, can you dance like this?

16

Dab

Hold one arm out straight to the side. Bend the other at the elbow, so that the hand is by your opposite shoulder. Dip your head so that your face is hidden behind the bent elbow. This is the dab—hold it for a moment, then go on to your next move.

START

FINISH!

⑰ Pool noodle tunnel

Cut four swimming pool noodles in half, and bend them into semicircles. Arrange them to make a tunnel. Secure the ends of the noodles by using tent pegs to attach them to the ground (don't do this one indoors!).

Crawl through the pool noodle tunnel on your hands and knees, making sure you don't touch it.

㉒ Hoop run

Lay out five Hula-Hoops on the ground, leading to the finish. Step into the first hoop, and lift it up and over your body before putting it back down. Repeat this with the four hoops left.

MAKE YOUR OWN OBSTACLE COURSE

The best place to set up an **obstacle course** is an **open space**, such as a yard, park, or large room. Here are a few **ideas** to get you started. How quickly can you make it to the end?

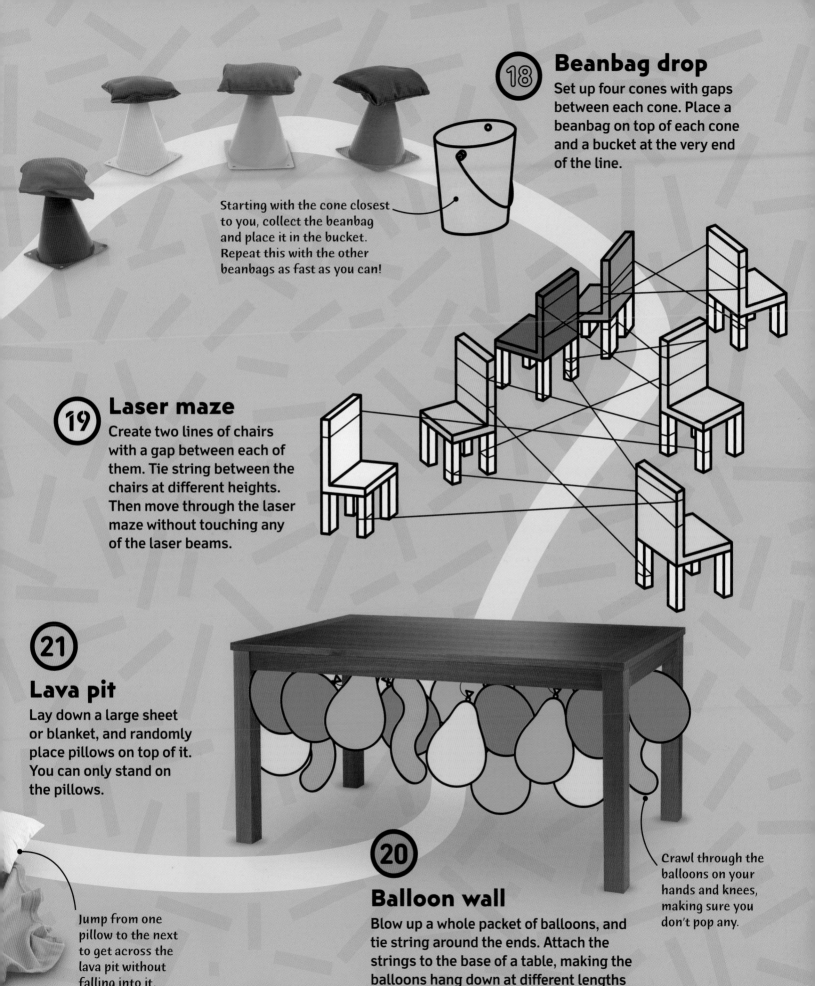

18 Beanbag drop

Set up four cones with gaps between each cone. Place a beanbag on top of each cone and a bucket at the very end of the line.

Starting with the cone closest to you, collect the beanbag and place it in the bucket. Repeat this with the other beanbags as fast as you can!

19 Laser maze

Create two lines of chairs with a gap between each of them. Tie string between the chairs at different heights. Then move through the laser maze without touching any of the laser beams.

21 Lava pit

Lay down a large sheet or blanket, and randomly place pillows on top of it. You can only stand on the pillows.

Jump from one pillow to the next to get across the lava pit without falling into it.

20 Balloon wall

Blow up a whole packet of balloons, and tie string around the ends. Attach the strings to the base of a table, making the balloons hang down at different lengths to create a wall.

Crawl through the balloons on your hands and knees, making sure you don't pop any.

MAKE LEMONADE

 STEP 1 Making lemonade is simple. First cut five lemons in half and squeeze all of the juice out into a large bowl or container.

STEP 2 Next add ½ cup (100 g) of sugar and 2 cups (500 ml) of water, and stir together until the sugar has dissolved.

STEP 3 Chill in the fridge for a couple of hours, then serve! Add mint leaves for extra flavor.

 ## ALSO TRY

If you want to be adventurous with your flavors, you could add other fruit to your recipe. Try crushing raspberries or using limes instead of lemons.

MAKE A LEMONADE STAND

A lemonade stand is a great way to start your first business. Sell your **freshly made** lemonade, and donate the money you make to your **favorite charity**!

Make sure you have a stash of extra cups.

! ALWAYS ASK AN ADULT TO HELP YOU SET UP YOUR LEMONADE STAND IN A SAFE PLACE.

Find a good selling spot

Your lemonade stand needs to be somewhere you can attract a lot of attention.

Tasty lemonade here!

All proceeds go to charity!

Attract customers

Make sure people know you're there! Be loud and friendly.

Make a money box

Keep your earnings in a box. You may need to start off with some change in case people don't have the correct money.

Use your earnings

Make sure you tell your customers which charity the money will go to. At the end of the day, count up how much you've earned, then donate it. Give yourself a pat on the back!

FRESH LEMONADE

$1 PER GLASS

Make sure customers know the price of your lemonade.

Make a sign

Create a simple sign that lets everyone know what you're selling and how much it costs.

PUPPET SHOW

There are plenty of fun ways you can make **puppets**.
Once you've made a few, it's time to put on a show.
Construct a homemade **theater**, gather your **audience**,
and put on an unforgettable **performance**!

㉖ Sock puppet

An old sock is all you need to make a simple puppet. Stick two googly eyes onto the base of the sock, and then place your hand inside. Move your fingers and thumb up and down to make the puppet talk.

㉕ Paper puppets

⚠ With a bit of paper and some imagination you can make all sorts of cool puppets. Cut holes in the bottom, and use your fingers as legs!

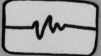

Duck behind a table, and balance your fingers on the surface.

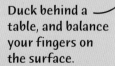

Try to keep your fingers straight.

Some of the puppets could have holes for four fingers.

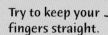

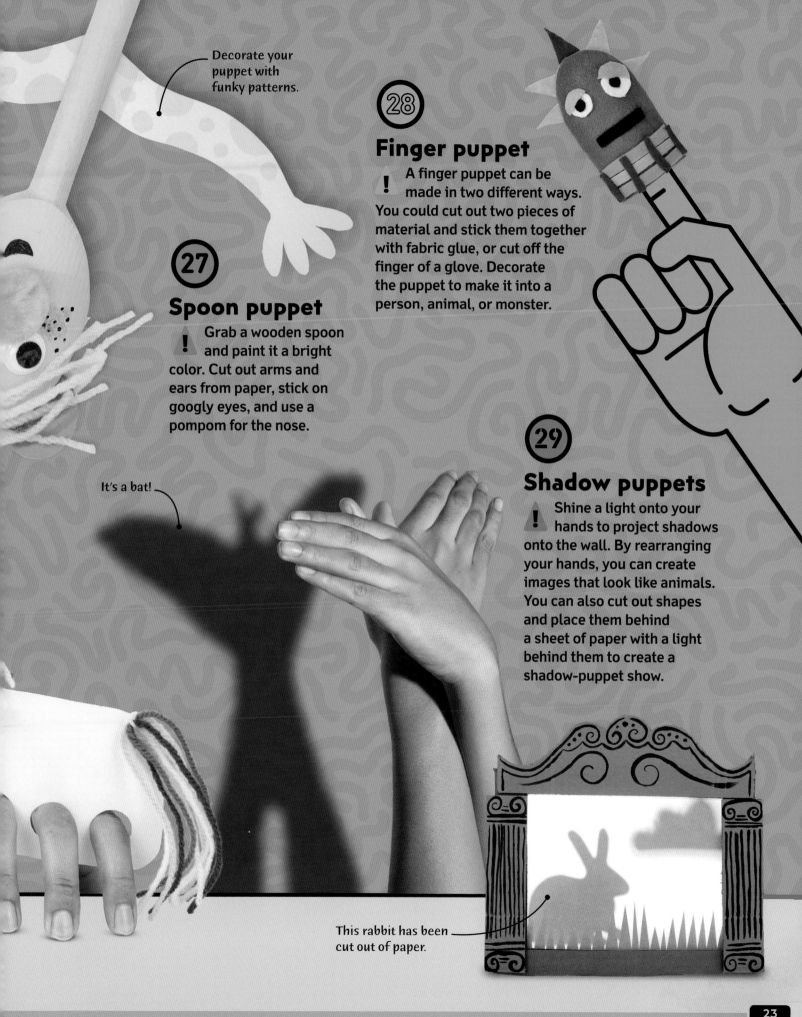

Decorate your puppet with funky patterns.

28 Finger puppet

! A finger puppet can be made in two different ways. You could cut out two pieces of material and stick them together with fabric glue, or cut off the finger of a glove. Decorate the puppet to make it into a person, animal, or monster.

27 Spoon puppet

! Grab a wooden spoon and paint it a bright color. Cut out arms and ears from paper, stick on googly eyes, and use a pompom for the nose.

It's a bat!

29 Shadow puppets

! Shine a light onto your hands to project shadows onto the wall. By rearranging your hands, you can create images that look like animals. You can also cut out shapes and place them behind a sheet of paper with a light behind them to create a shadow-puppet show.

This rabbit has been cut out of paper.

FRUIT MONSTERS!

⚠ Feeling hungry? These **monstrous artworks** are all made from fruit, so they **taste** as good as they **look**. You will **need an adult** to help you cut up the different fruits.

㉚ Penguin Polly

STEP 1 Take a medium-sized banana, and cut a quarter off its end so that it can stand up.

TOP TIP
Remember to wash your hands before you start!

STEP 2 Peel the banana's skin up on three sides, and cut off the front peel to make the penguin's belly.

STEP 3 Cut two foot shapes from the tops of oranges, and place them in front of the banana. Then poke two toothpicks with raisins on them into the top of the banana to make eyes.

㉛ Fruity Fred

STEP 1 Carefully cut three holes into your pear, as shown here. These will be Fred's eyes and mouth.

STEP 2 Put two small fruits, such as raspberries or raisins, into the eye holes. Then add some sunflower seeds to give your monster teeth.

Cut a piece of orange peel for the tongue.

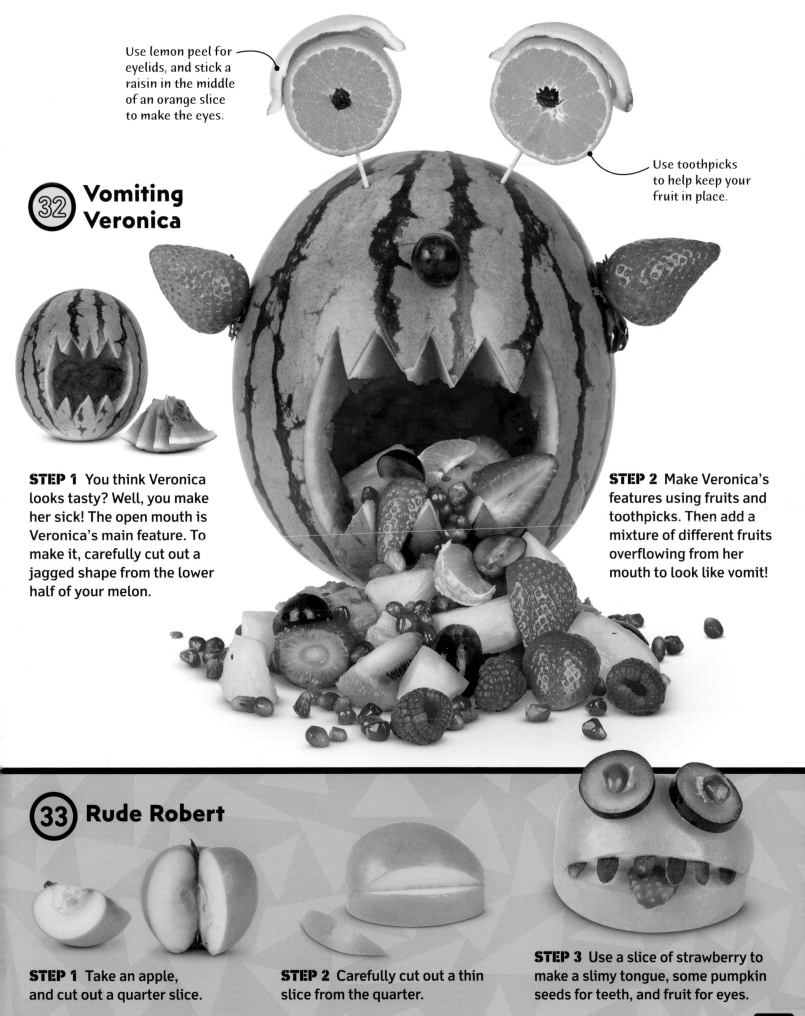

Use lemon peel for eyelids, and stick a raisin in the middle of an orange slice to make the eyes.

Use toothpicks to help keep your fruit in place.

(32) Vomiting Veronica

STEP 1 You think Veronica looks tasty? Well, you make her sick! The open mouth is Veronica's main feature. To make it, carefully cut out a jagged shape from the lower half of your melon.

STEP 2 Make Veronica's features using fruits and toothpicks. Then add a mixture of different fruits overflowing from her mouth to look like vomit!

(33) Rude Robert

STEP 1 Take an apple, and cut out a quarter slice.

STEP 2 Carefully cut out a thin slice from the quarter.

STEP 3 Use a slice of strawberry to make a slimy tongue, some pumpkin seeds for teeth, and fruit for eyes.

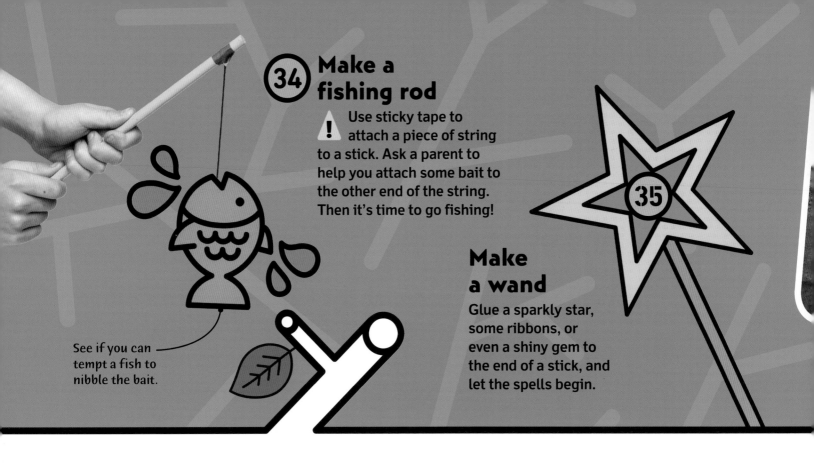

34 Make a fishing rod

! Use sticky tape to attach a piece of string to a stick. Ask a parent to help you attach some bait to the other end of the string. Then it's time to go fishing!

See if you can tempt a fish to nibble the bait.

Make a wand

Glue a sparkly star, some ribbons, or even a shiny gem to the end of a stick, and let the spells begin.

35

THINGS TO DO WITH...

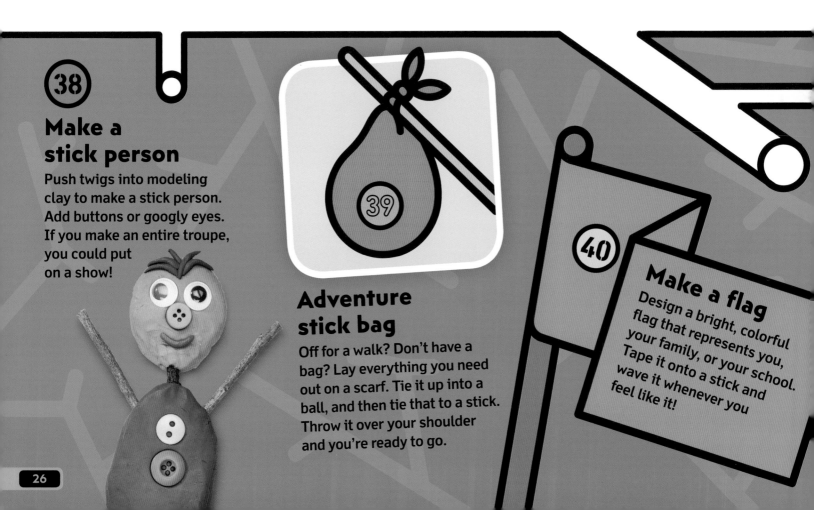

38 Make a stick person

Push twigs into modeling clay to make a stick person. Add buttons or googly eyes. If you make an entire troupe, you could put on a show!

39 Adventure stick bag

Off for a walk? Don't have a bag? Lay everything you need out on a scarf. Tie it up into a ball, and then tie that to a stick. Throw it over your shoulder and you're ready to go.

40 Make a flag

Design a bright, colorful flag that represents you, your family, or your school. Tape it onto a stick and wave it whenever you feel like it!

36 Race them

When you're near a stream with your friends, find a stick each and throw them from one side of a bridge. See which one floats to the other side of the bridge first.

Do you think a bigger stick will be faster?

37 Play pick-up sticks

Get a handful of small sticks. Drop them on the floor, and take turns trying to remove each one without disturbing the others. If you fail, it's the end of your turn. Who has the most sticks at the end?

A STICK!

41 Build a den

Want a place to read? Or hide out? Or take a nap? Then you need a den. Gather lots of different sized branches for this sticky challenge. (No glue required.)

Rest your largest branch on two sturdy branches.

Prop other pairs of branches up against your main branch.

Cover your den in grass or leaves.

42 Stick relay

Get into two teams and have a stick relay race! Each person has to run a short distance before passing the stick to the next in line. Which team can get to the end first?

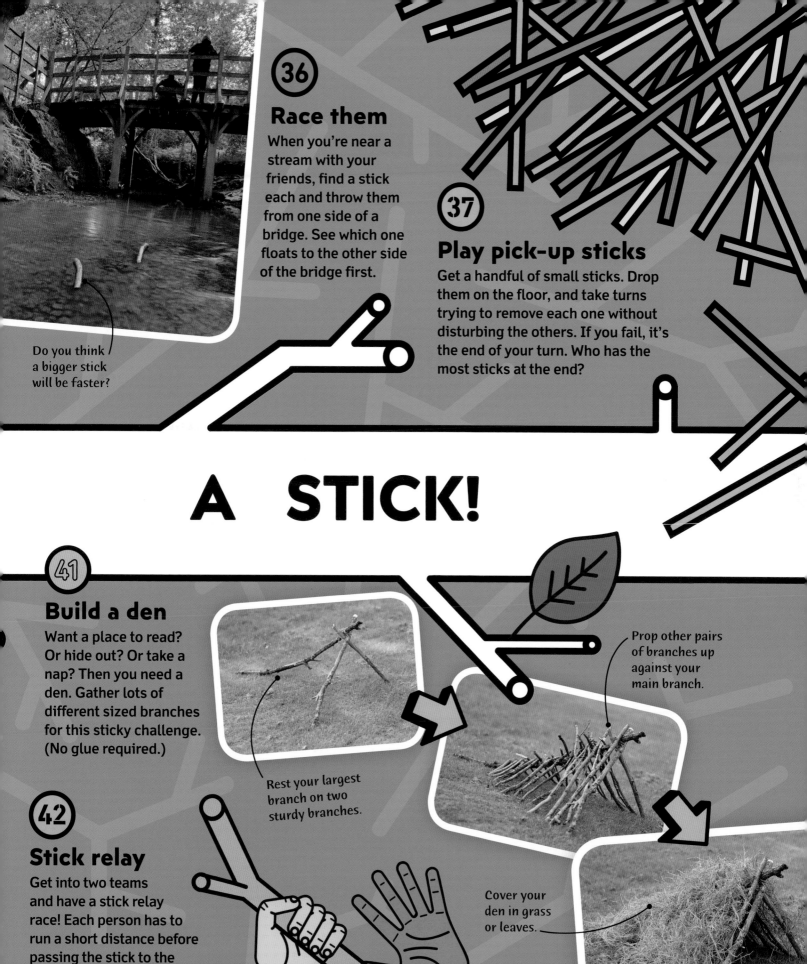

CREATE A CLUB

Clubs are groups where you can get together with **friends** who have similar **interests** to you. You could talk about your favorite books or play board games. If you have a quiet afternoon to spare, you could **start a club** of your own. Here are some ideas to get you started.

43 Find a clubhouse

Your club will need somewhere to meet. Find a good place to set up your clubhouse. It could be in a tree house, under a bunk bed, or behind a couch. Decorate it with comfy pillows and things to do with your club, such as books, posters, and toys.

44 Secret handshake

A secret handshake is a way for members of your club to greet one another without anyone else knowing. Put together a sequence of moves that only your club knows—for example: shake hands, snap your fingers, turn around, then fist bump. The more complicated the better!

NO ADULTS!

TOP TIP
Clubs are no fun if people are left out—except for the adults! Ask anyone who is interested if they want to join.

(45)

Make membership cards
Many clubs give their members membership cards. You can make yours using cardboard, coloring pencils, and glue. Include the member's name, membership number, and a photograph or drawing of them.

THE SPY CLUB

Name:
James

Membership no.
007

STARTING A CLUB
Think about what sort of club you would like to start. What are your hobbies? Who might like to join your club?

FOSSIL FRIENDS

THE ASTRONOMY CLUB

Do you like looking at the night sky? Start an astronomy club!

COMEDY CLUB

SCIENCE SQUAD

In a science club, you could perform experiments.

SKATEBOARD CLUB

DRAMA CLUB

Kids' kitchen

Appetizer
Delicious rice salad with peppers, green onions, sweet corn, and pomegranate seeds

Entrée
Amazing pizza faces

Dessert
Mouth-watering ice-cream sundae

46

Write a menu

Before your restaurant opens for business, you need to write a menu for your customers. This will tell them exactly what food they'll be eating for each course.

Think of a fun name for your restaurant, and write it at the top of the menu.

Make each course sound appetizing. You want people to come and eat at your restaurant!

You could even draw pictures of what the dishes will look like.

Use broccoli florets for the hair.

A slice of bell pepper creates the perfect smile.

47

Prepare food

Prepare the food before your guests arrive so you don't have to do too many things once they've sat down. Here are a few simple recipes you could try.

! Rice salad

STEP 1 Ask an adult to boil a portion of rice or heat up a packet of pre-cooked rice.

STEP 2 Cut bell peppers and green onions into small slices. An adult should help you to do this, too.

STEP 3 Mix the rice, peppers, and green onions in a bowl. Add pomegranate seeds and sweet corn. You're good to go!

Eyes can be made out of slices of courgette and olives.

TOP TIP
Make sure you check if your customers have any allergies. Avoid food that may be dangerous for them to eat.

⚠ Pizza faces

STEP 1 Buy pre-made pizza bases, and cover the tops of them in tomato sauce.

STEP 2 Use ingredients, such as cheese, bell peppers, and tomatoes, to decorate your pizzas like faces.

STEP 3 Bake in the oven for eight to ten minutes. Once they're cooked, use oven gloves to take them out.

Super sundae

STEP 1 Decide what ice-cream flavors you want in your sundae. Chocolate, vanilla, and strawberry make a great combination.

STEP 2 In a bowl or sundae glass, serve up three or four scoops on top of one another.

STEP 3 Add toppings, such as colorful sprinkles and nuts, and finish with a drizzle of caramel sauce.

OPEN A RESTAURANT

⚠ Fruity feast

STEP 1 Choose a selection of fruit, such as strawberries, raspberries, oranges, kiwis, and grapes.

STEP 2 Ask an adult to help you cut the fruit up.

STEP 3 Mix all the fruit together in a bowl, and serve up your fruity feast.

 (48)

Play server

Be friendly and polite to your customers when taking their orders. They might even give you a tip at the end!

ARE WE THERE YET?

 I spy

This is a guessing game. One person starts by saying, "I spy with my little eye, something beginning with…" They fill the gap at the end with the first letter of an object they have seen out the window. The other players then try to guess what the word is. Whoever gets it right goes next. This is a great one to play in a traffic jam!

51 Association game

The first player starts by saying a word. Then everyone takes turns adding words that are associated with the last word that was said. For example: lettuce, leaf, tree, bird, egg. Say the first thing that comes into your head. If you hesitate for too long or repeat a word, you're out!

52 Counting game

The aim of this game is to count from 1 to 20. Each person can say up to three numbers at a time. Because players don't know when other people are about to speak, sometimes they will talk over one another. Each time this happens, everyone has to start again from one.

 Storytelling

In this game, you make up your own story. The first person starts by saying "Once upon a time…" Players then take turns adding sentences to the story. The story can be as long as you like. They often end up being strange because everyone has very different ideas!

 **Alphabet game**

Start by choosing a category such as animals, cars, names, or food. The players must go through the alphabet and name as many things from that category as they can. Start with A, then move on to B, C, D, and so on. If someone can't think of anything beginning with a letter, they are out.

Being in the **car** for a long time can get **boring**. Here are some **games** you can play **on the road**. You won't need anything other than your brain and some other passengers to play with.

54 Word game
The first person starts by saying a word. The next person has to say a word that starts with the last letter of the previous word. For example: banan**a**, **a**naconda, **a**n**t**, **t**ool**s**, **s**cissors.

55 Name that tune
Each passenger takes turns humming a song or theme song. The other players must try to guess the tune. Try not to make it too difficult.

56 I went to the store...
This game tests your memory. Someone starts by saying "I went to the store, and I bought…"—ending with something they bought. The next player repeats the sentence, including what the last person bought, and adds another item to the list. Every item added to the list has to be remembered and repeated back. Keep playing until someone gets it wrong!

TOP TIP
You don't have to stick to things you can buy in actual stores. Maybe you'd like to buy an elephant or a time machine?

Box arch

Cut out a door shape on opposite sides of a cardboard box. Then try to hit your ball through the hole without touching the box.

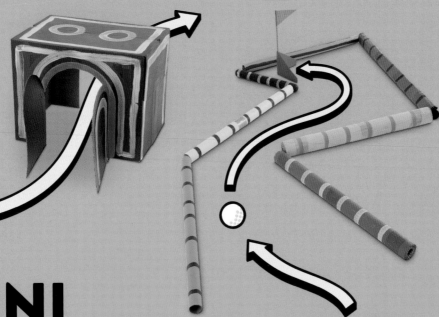

Walls

Build mini golf walls using umbrellas, rolling pins, or garden sticks. If you don't have these items, make your own by rolling cardboard into tubes and sticking them together. To create bends in your walls, place the items at different angles—this will make the course trickier.

(57) MINI GOLF

⚠️ In mini golf, you have to get your ball past various **funky obstacles** to the holes at the end. The aim is to get around the course in the **least number** of shots. You can try building your very own **mini golf course**.

Golf "holes" can be simple cardboard targets.

Plant pot bridges

Place two plant pots slightly apart from each other. Make them into a bridge by placing a book on top. Now try to knock your ball through the bridge.

If you cut a window out of the top of the tube, you can see your ball roll down.

Wiggle frames

Fold a strip of cardboard down at either end and stand it up. Make four of these wiggle frames and line them up in a row. Try to hit your ball through all of them in one try. Angling them will make it harder.

Tunnel ramp

To make a tunnel ramp, take a long piece of cardboard and prop it up on a box. Then add a long cardboard tube to the other side. Add walls to the ramp to help guide your ball.

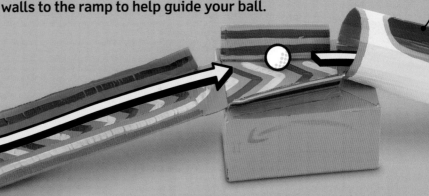

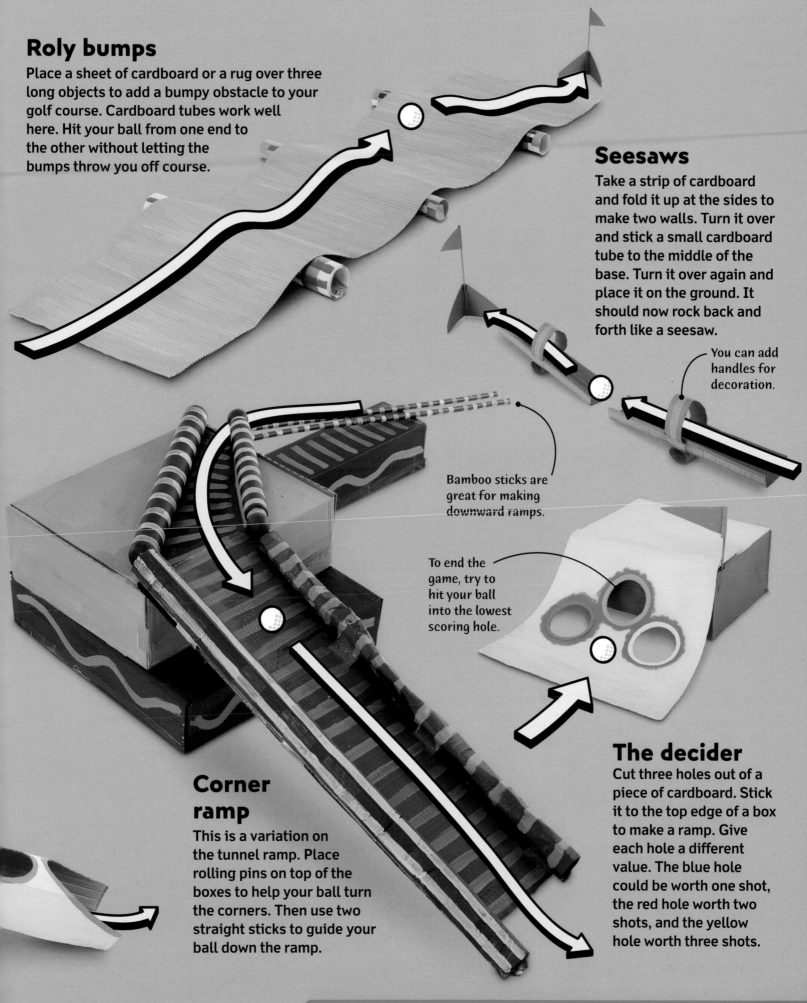

Roly bumps

Place a sheet of cardboard or a rug over three long objects to add a bumpy obstacle to your golf course. Cardboard tubes work well here. Hit your ball from one end to the other without letting the bumps throw you off course.

Seesaws

Take a strip of cardboard and fold it up at the sides to make two walls. Turn it over and stick a small cardboard tube to the middle of the base. Turn it over again and place it on the ground. It should now rock back and forth like a seesaw.

You can add handles for decoration.

Bamboo sticks are great for making downward ramps.

To end the game, try to hit your ball into the lowest scoring hole.

Corner ramp

This is a variation on the tunnel ramp. Place rolling pins on top of the boxes to help your ball turn the corners. Then use two straight sticks to guide your ball down the ramp.

The decider

Cut three holes out of a piece of cardboard. Stick it to the top edge of a box to make a ramp. Give each hole a different value. The blue hole could be worth one shot, the red hole worth two shots, and the yellow hole worth three shots.

Turn the page to find out how to put your course together.

MAKE A CLUB

All you need is a stick and some cardboard!

Wrap a strip of cardboard around the tip of the stick to make a handle.

Add cardboard to the bottom to make the head of the club.

Make sure there aren't any gaps in your walls so the ball can't escape.

Hit the ball with a bit of force to push it up the ramp.

Add or remove tubes from the bumpy alley to make it harder or easier.

Start here
Decide what obstacle you want to start with, and position it at the beginning of your course.

...MAKE A COURSE

Now that you've made all of your **obstacles**, position them in whatever order you like to complete your **mini golf course**. Give it a **test run**, and then make any adjustments.

TOP TIP
Paint your obstacles in all sorts of colors and patterns to make them really stand out!

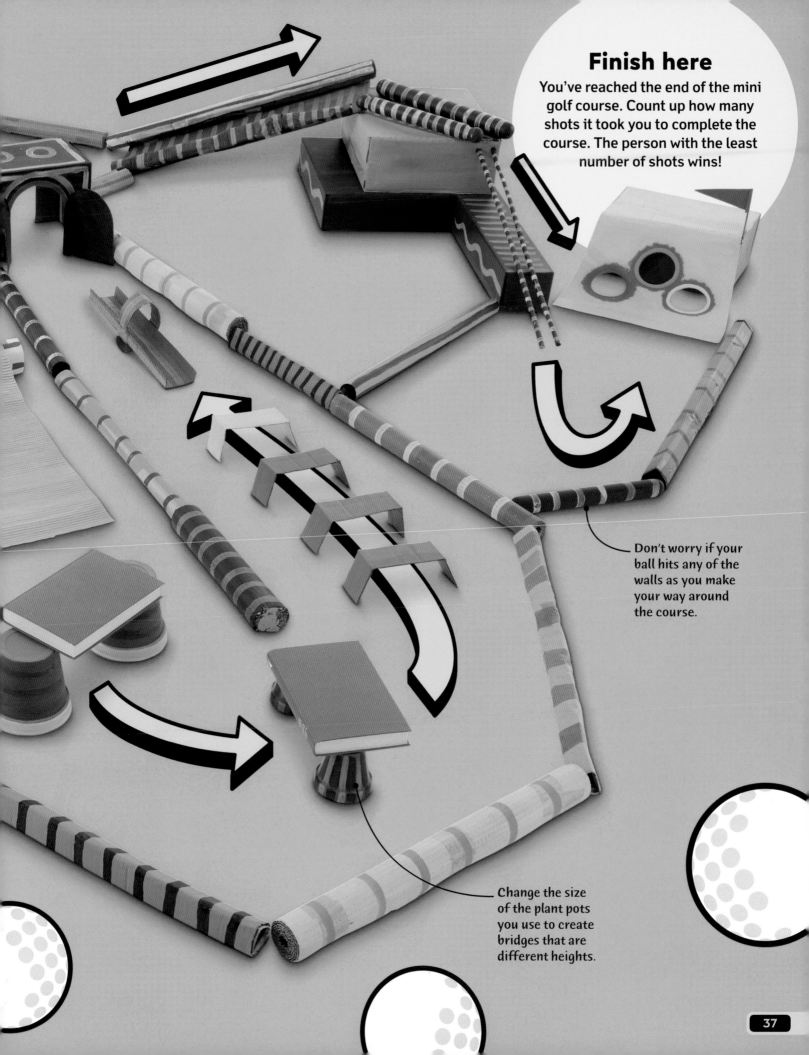

Finish here

You've reached the end of the mini golf course. Count up how many shots it took you to complete the course. The person with the least number of shots wins!

Don't worry if your ball hits any of the walls as you make your way around the course.

Change the size of the plant pots you use to create bridges that are different heights.

58 PLAY CHECKERS

Checkers is an **excellent** first board game to learn to play. It is incredibly simple, but it's rare that two games are the same. You'll need a **checkerboard and pieces** in order to play this game.

Black pieces always go first.

There are 12 pieces on each side.

To start

Line up your pieces on the 12 black squares nearest to you. The aim is to capture all of your opponent's pieces before they capture yours. The game is only played on the black squares.

DID YOU KNOW?

Checkers is called draughts in some countries.

A simple move

Take turns moving one piece at a time. A simple move consists of moving your piece in a diagonal direction to the nearest black square. Regular checkers pieces can only move forward.

Taking pieces

To take one of your opponent's pieces, you have to jump it. You can only jump an opponent's piece if your piece is next to it and there is a free space on the other side. You can jump more than one piece in one move—if it's possible! If you can take a piece, you HAVE TO TAKE IT. Failure to do so results in your piece being removed from the board.

This piece can move diagonally one space to the left or right.

This piece is being jumped.

The attacking piece ends up on the other side of the piece it has taken.

King me!

If you manage to get one of your pieces to your opponent's side of the board, it becomes a king. To crown your king, you stack one of your taken pieces on top of it. A king is a very important piece—it can move forward and backward.

To win

The game ends when one player has successfully taken all of their opponent's pieces. It is a game of skill and strategy. The best players will use the "have to take" rule to lay traps for their opponent, sacrificing their own pieces in order to put them in a better position.

59 PLAY CHESS

In this two-player game, you use **skill** and **strategy** to try to outwit your opponent. You'll need a **chessboard and pieces** in order to play this game.

Each square is identified by a number and a letter— for example, a6.

To start

Position the board so that there is a white square on each player's bottom-right corner. Set up the pieces in the exact positions they are shown here.

The white queen always starts on a white square, and the black queen always starts on a black square.

Pawn

Each player starts with eight pawns. They line up on the second and seventh rows. Pawns can move one or two squares forward from their starting position, but only one square forward after that.

Pawns move one square diagonally forward to capture a piece. Otherwise, they can only move forward.

Knight

Each player has two knights. They are positioned on squares b1 and g1, and b8 and g8. Knights are the only pieces that can jump over other pieces. They can move three squares in an "L" shape.

Knights can only move horizontally and vertically. They always move in an "L" shape.

Bishop

Each player has two bishops. They are positioned on squares c1 and f1, and c8 and f8. Bishops can move any number of squares diagonally.

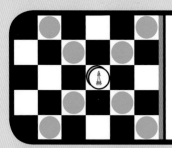

Bishops can only move diagonally. They can move any number of squares.

Rook

Each player has two rooks, or castles. They are positioned on squares a1 and h1, and a8 and h8. Rooks can move any number of squares up or down, or to either side.

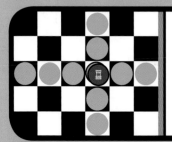

Rooks can move forward, backward, or sideway, but not diagonally. They can move any number of squares.

Queen

Each player has one queen. They are positioned on squares d1 and d8. Queens can move any number of squares in any direction. They are the most powerful piece.

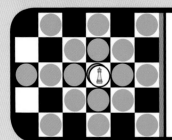

Queens can move any number of squares in straight lines in any direction.

King

Each player has one king. They are positioned on squares e1 and e8. Kings can move one square. The aim of the game is to checkmate your opponent's king (see page 42).

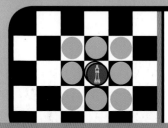

Kings can move one square in any direction. They can never be captured.

Turn the page to find out how to play!

AIM OF THE GAME

Capture!

Victory will be yours if you can capture your opponent's pieces and ultimately checkmate their king (see below). To capture the other player's chess pieces, move one of your pieces into a square that contains one of their pieces. You can only capture one piece at a time. Pieces that have been captured are removed from the board.

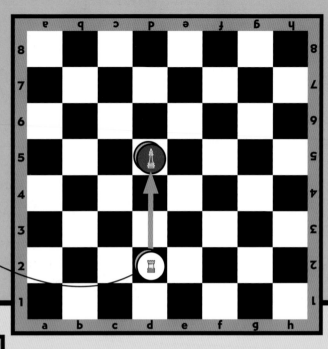

The white rook can capture the black bishop.

The white bishop has put the black king in check. Black can escape check by capturing the white bishop with the knight, blocking check by moving the pawn to c6, or moving the king to a safe square.

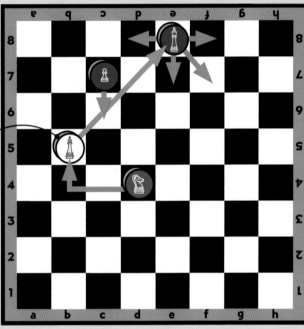

Check!

When your king is attacked, it is "in check." You MUST escape from check, by either:

1. Capturing the piece that put the king in check

2. Blocking the check with another piece

3. Moving the king to a safe square

Remember—you can never capture a king!

Checkmate!

Checkmate ends the game. If your king is in check and cannot escape from check immediately, then it is checkmate and you have lost.

The white queen has checkmated the black king. Black cannot capture the queen, no black piece can block the check, and the king cannot move to escape from check. Game over!

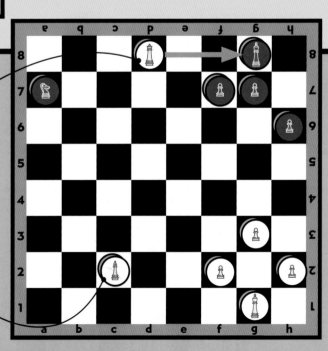

The king can't move to h7 because the white bishop would put it in check.

PLAYING THE GAME

To start the game
The player with the white pieces always moves first. Flip a coin to decide who is white. The players then take turns to move until a winner is crowned.

Players usually start by moving a pawn.

Capturing your opponent's pieces
Try to capture as many of your opponent's pieces as possible. Make sure you don't forget to protect your own pieces while you're capturing others.

You have to make a move each turn, even if it puts your pieces in danger.

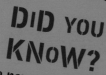

DID YOU KNOW?
If a pawn reaches the opposite side of the board, it is immediately promoted to a more important piece—anything except for a king. Most of the time a queen is chosen.

Winning the game
In order to win a game of chess, you must checkmate your opponent's king. This is easier to do if you've captured a lot of your opponent's pieces already, leaving their king unprotected.

Value of pieces
Each piece is given a value, so you know how important it is. The little pawns are only worth 1 point, while the mighty queen is worth 9 points. If you do not have time to finish a game with checkmate, games can be decided by who has captured the most points.

Pawn: 1

Knight: 3

Bishop: 3

Rook: 5

Queen: 9

King: You can never capture a king, so it doesn't have a value!

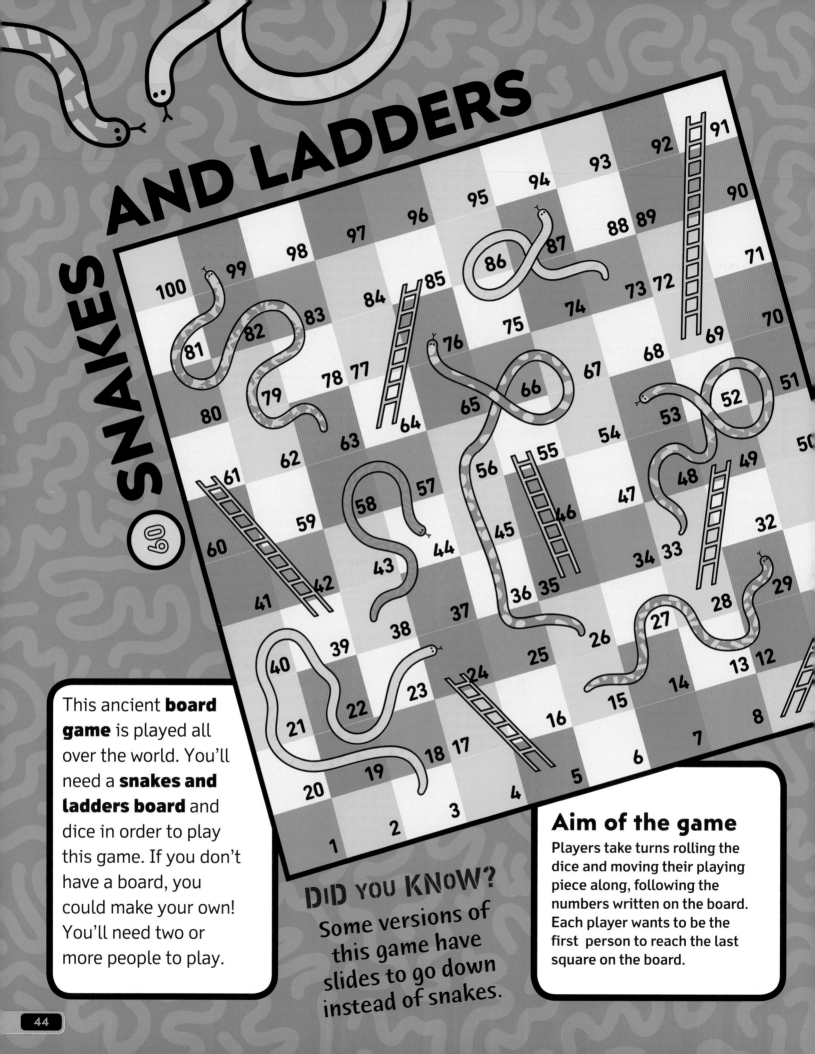

SNAKES AND LADDERS

This ancient **board game** is played all over the world. You'll need a **snakes and ladders board** and dice in order to play this game. If you don't have a board, you could make your own! You'll need two or more people to play.

DID YOU KNOW?
Some versions of this game have slides to go down instead of snakes.

Aim of the game
Players take turns rolling the dice and moving their playing piece along, following the numbers written on the board. Each player wants to be the first person to reach the last square on the board.

THE RULES

Start the game

Each person chooses a playing piece. They decide who goes first by rolling the dice—whoever gets the highest number starts. Now you can start playing. Take turns rolling the dice and moving your playing pieces along by the number you rolled.

Up the ladders

If you land on a square that has the bottom of a ladder on it, you can climb up the ladder to the top. If you land on the middle or the top of a ladder, you stay where you are. You never move down a ladder.

Down the snakes

If you land on a square that has a snake's head on it, you slide down the snake to the end of its tail. If you land on the middle or the bottom of a snake, you stay where you are. You never move up a snake.

Winning the game

To win, you must roll the exact number needed to land on the final square. So, if you are three squares away, you must roll 3 to win. If you rolled 4, you would have to move your piece along three steps, but then move back one step.

GAME HISTORY

Snakes and ladders was invented in India. Originally the game was about good and bad. A player's movement along the board represented a life journey complicated by good things (ladders) and bad ones (snakes).

TRY THIS

Here are some different ways to play the game:

- To speed the game up, change the ending so that you don't have to throw an exact number to land on the final square.

- Try playing with two playing pieces each! Each time you roll the dice, you must choose which of your pieces to move. The aim is to get both pieces to the final square first.

- Add another danger: If someone lands on a square with another person's piece on it, that person has to start again!

61 INVENT YOUR OWN BOARD GAME

If you enjoy **playing board games** with your friends and family, why not try making your **own game**? Put on your **thinking cap** as we help you figure out how to make the best board game around.

Choose a theme

Decide what theme you'd like your game to have. Is it a pirate game or a game with witches and wizards? This will help you decide how to decorate the board. For example, a pirate game could have a treasure chest on the final square!

Aim of the game

Many board games have a path for people to follow that leads them to the winning square. If you decide to have a path, give it lots of twists and turns. Make sure it's easy to follow with a clear beginning and end.

It might be that if you land on a particular square, you have to loop back to an earlier one!

START

Brainstorm ideas

Get together with friends and think about what kind of game you'd like to make. You might start by thinking about your favorite board games, and use some elements from them in your new game.

Game pieces need to be different colors or shapes.

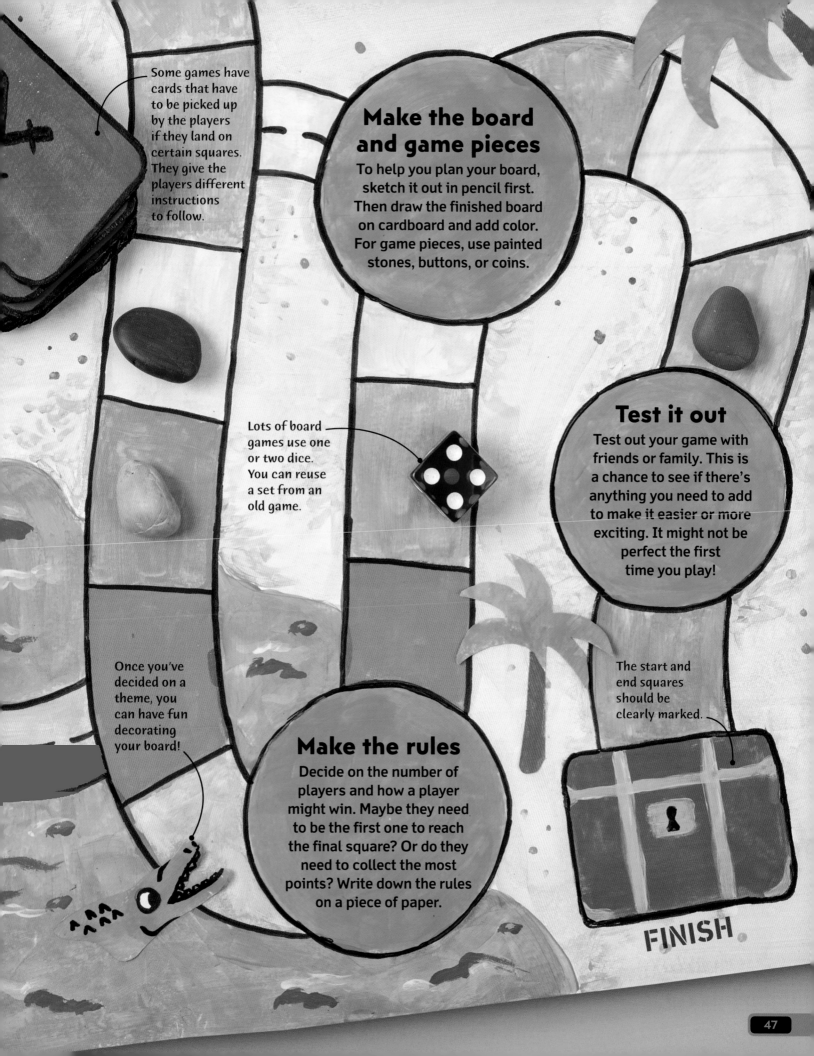

Some games have cards that have to be picked up by the players if they land on certain squares. They give the players different instructions to follow.

Make the board and game pieces

To help you plan your board, sketch it out in pencil first. Then draw the finished board on cardboard and add color. For game pieces, use painted stones, buttons, or coins.

Lots of board games use one or two dice. You can reuse a set from an old game.

Test it out

Test out your game with friends or family. This is a chance to see if there's anything you need to add to make it easier or more exciting. It might not be perfect the first time you play!

Once you've decided on a theme, you can have fun decorating your board!

The start and end squares should be clearly marked.

Make the rules

Decide on the number of players and how a player might win. Maybe they need to be the first one to reach the final square? Or do they need to collect the most points? Write down the rules on a piece of paper.

FINISH

62 Skipping stones

Find a smooth, flat stone and try skipping it across the surface of a river, lake, or pond. See how many times you can get it to bounce on the water before it sinks.

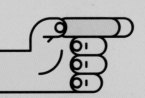

63 Picture frame

Why not make an unusual stony frame for a special picture? All you need is strong glue, a collection of small stones, and some cardboard to stick them on.

THINGS TO DO WITH...

66 Stone cactus

Create a cactus by painting a stone. Use different colors and patterns to make it look realistic. You could even "plant" it with other "cacti" in a pot!

67 Rock art

Play around with stones to see what shapes and pictures you can create. If you arrange them carefully, you could produce an artistic masterpiece.

68 Paperweight

Stones make great paperweights to hold things down. Decorate them by gluing loops of colorful string around the stones.

64 Game pieces

Brightly painted stones make great game pieces. You could use them to play board games, such as snakes and ladders (see pages 44–45).

65 Domino stones

Make your own dominoes—here are the patterns you'll need. Each player takes seven pieces. The person with the highest double—for example, 6-6—goes first. The next player must put down a domino with a matching side, such as 6-4. The matching sides always need to be touching. Players keep going until they have no dominoes left. If you can't go, you must pick up another domino.

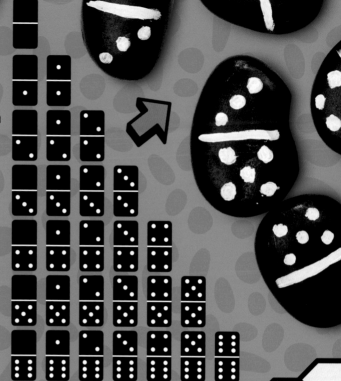

A STONE!

69 Towers

Collect stones and see how many you can stack on top of one another. Have a stacking competition with your friends!

70 Painted pebbles

With a bit of paint, you can turn your stones into animals or give them cool patterns. Add pipe cleaners, felt, buttons, or googly eyes for added decoration.

71 Rock collection

How many different looking rocks can you find? Store your specimens neatly in cardboard tubes so you can compare them.

⑦2 GROW A PLANT

STEP 1 It's easy to grow your own food! Start with empty eggshells that have had their tops cut off. Fill them with some fluffy cotton.

STEP 2 Scatter cress seeds on top. If you don't have cress seeds, you can use wheat seeds instead.

STEP 3 Water the seeds. You will need to keep the cotton moist at all times. Put the eggshells on a sunny windowsill. After a few days, you should see cress sprouting.

⑦3 Decorate the egg
Add smiley faces to your eggshells. Once the cress starts growing, it will look like the eggshells have hair!

HOW DO PLANTS GROW?

Most plants begin as seeds. Seeds contain the instructions for making the baby plant.

When the temperature is right and the seed has enough water, the plant will begin to emerge.

Eventually the plant reaches the surface, where it gets energy from sunlight and continues to grow.

(74) Harvest and eat

⚠ Once the cress is about 2 in (5 cm) tall, it is ready to harvest. Cut the stalks just above the cotton, and give the cress a rinse with water. Then add it to salads or sandwiches to give them a peppery flavor.

Learning **magic** is a great way to **amaze** your friends and family. Here are a few simple **tricks** to get you started. Remember— a good magician never reveals the **secrets** behind their tricks!

(75) Escapology

Magicians always seem to escape from impossible situations, but are they really as impossible as they seem? Here's how to escape from string handcuffs.

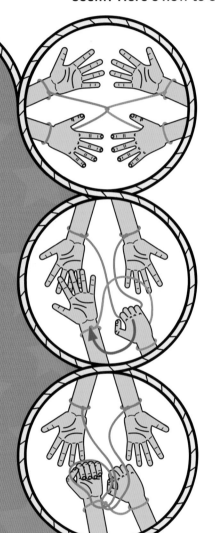

⚠ **STEP 1** Tie a loop of string around your wrists, but make sure it is not too tight. Ask a friend to do the same, but first cross your string over theirs.

STEP 2 Pull your friend's string toward you, then tuck it through the loop over your left hand from behind.

STEP 3 Bend your hand, and push it through the loop in your friend's string. Then straighten your hand.

STEP 4 Pull your hands away to free yourself!

TOP TIP
Come up with a really cool magician name to give you a mysterious air.

MAGIC

KING OF ESCAPES!

Harry Houdini lived from 1874 to 1926. He was able to escape from handcuffs, locked rooms, and padlocked chests! People still don't know how Houdini managed all his escapes.

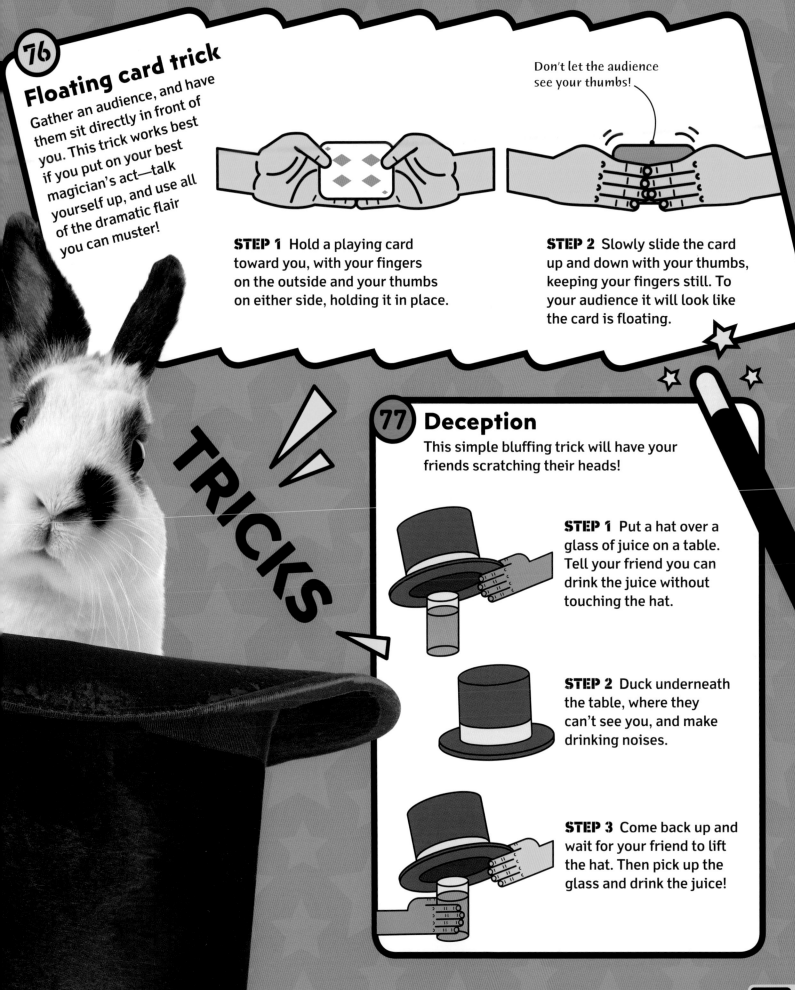

76 Floating card trick

Gather an audience, and have them sit directly in front of you. This trick works best if you put on your best magician's act—talk yourself up, and use all of the dramatic flair you can muster!

Don't let the audience see your thumbs!

STEP 1 Hold a playing card toward you, with your fingers on the outside and your thumbs on either side, holding it in place.

STEP 2 Slowly slide the card up and down with your thumbs, keeping your fingers still. To your audience it will look like the card is floating.

TRICKS

77 Deception

This simple bluffing trick will have your friends scratching their heads!

STEP 1 Put a hat over a glass of juice on a table. Tell your friend you can drink the juice without touching the hat.

STEP 2 Duck underneath the table, where they can't see you, and make drinking noises.

STEP 3 Come back up and wait for your friend to lift the hat. Then pick up the glass and drink the juice!

ILLUSIONS

Seeing isn't always believing. Our **eyes** can play **tricks** on us and make images appear confusing. Take a look at these illusions, and then see if you can **make your own**!

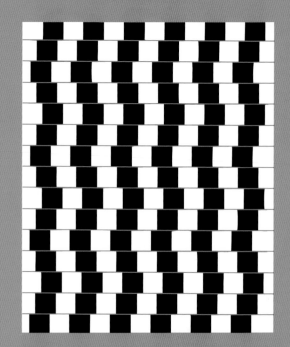

79 Wonky or straight?

Do the blue lines in this picture look wonky to you? Afraid not—they're all straight. This illusion is created because the black squares are not lined up next to one another, so our eyes think that the blue lines are crooked.

80 Two in one

What image can you see here? Two faces or a vase? Take a closer look—there are both!

Moving illusion

Look at this picture. Is it moving? The combination of black-and-white patterns makes this illusion look like it is, even though it's a completely still image.

⁸¹ DRAW YOUR OWN

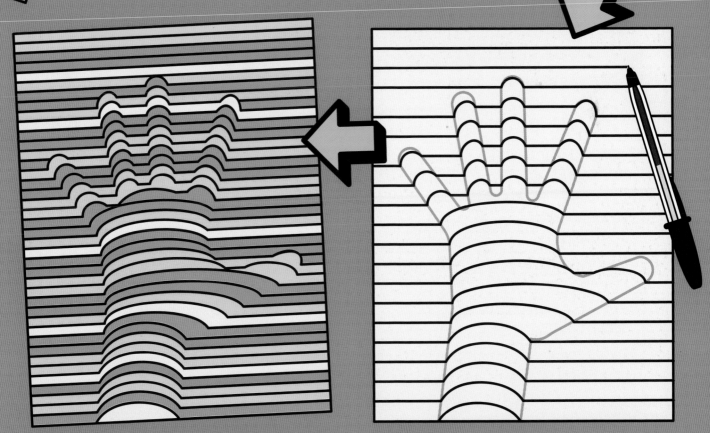

STEP 1 With a pencil, lightly trace around your hand on a piece of paper.

STEP 2 Use a black pen to draw a straight line from one edge of the paper to the other. Make sure the line doesn't cross over the outline of your hand.

STEP 3 Join the two straight lines together with a curved line. This will be inside the hand outline.

STEP 5 Fill in the spaces using different colors. Your picture should now look three-dimensional!

STEP 4 Repeat steps 2 and 3 for the rest of the drawing, leaving space between each line.

(82) FLOATING INK

When you draw with **ink**, it stays in the same place, right? Wrong! This fun **experiment** shows you how you can make your **drawings** come to **life**.

YOU WILL NEED

- ■ Dry-erase marker
- ■ Glass or ceramic plate
- ■ Cup of water

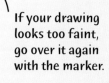

If your drawing looks too faint, go over it again with the marker.

STEP 1 Using a dry-erase marker, draw a stick person on your plate. Make sure all of the lines are connected and it's not too big. Now leave it to dry for a couple of seconds.

TOP TIP

Use a plain white plate for this trick so that you can clearly see your stick person.

STEP 2 Gently pour water onto your plate, but not directly onto the drawing. As the water covers the drawing, you should see it float to the surface!

STEP 3 Make your stick person dance! Blow on it, tip the water around, or gently push it with your fingers.

TRY DIFFERENT DESIGNS

This trick works with any drawing— it doesn't have to be a stick person. Try drawing animals, or give your stick person a balloon!

Which colors work best?

HOW IT WORKS

When you draw with a dry-erase marker, the ink dries into a thin, solid layer that is lighter than water. This means that when water is added, the drawing floats to the surface!

If you look closely, you'll be able to see the stick person slowly lifting up.

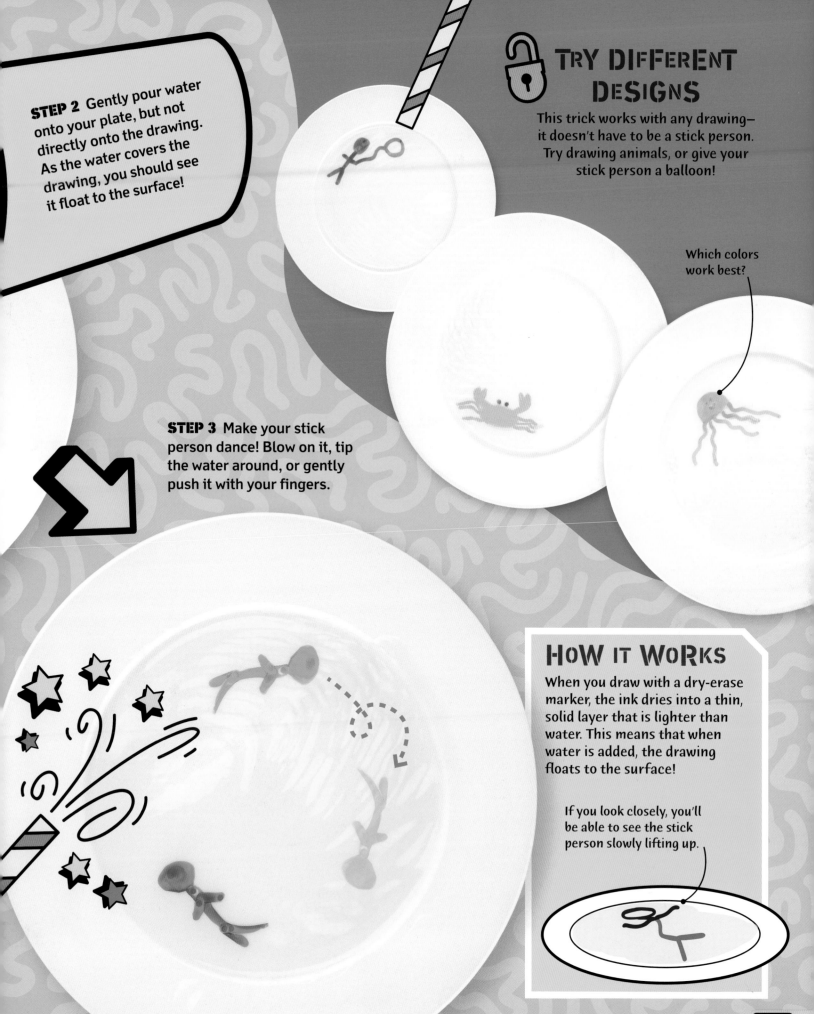

Do you want to host an **unforgettable party**? Follow these simple steps to **transform** your ordinary chairs into futuristic **robots** or amazing **animals**.

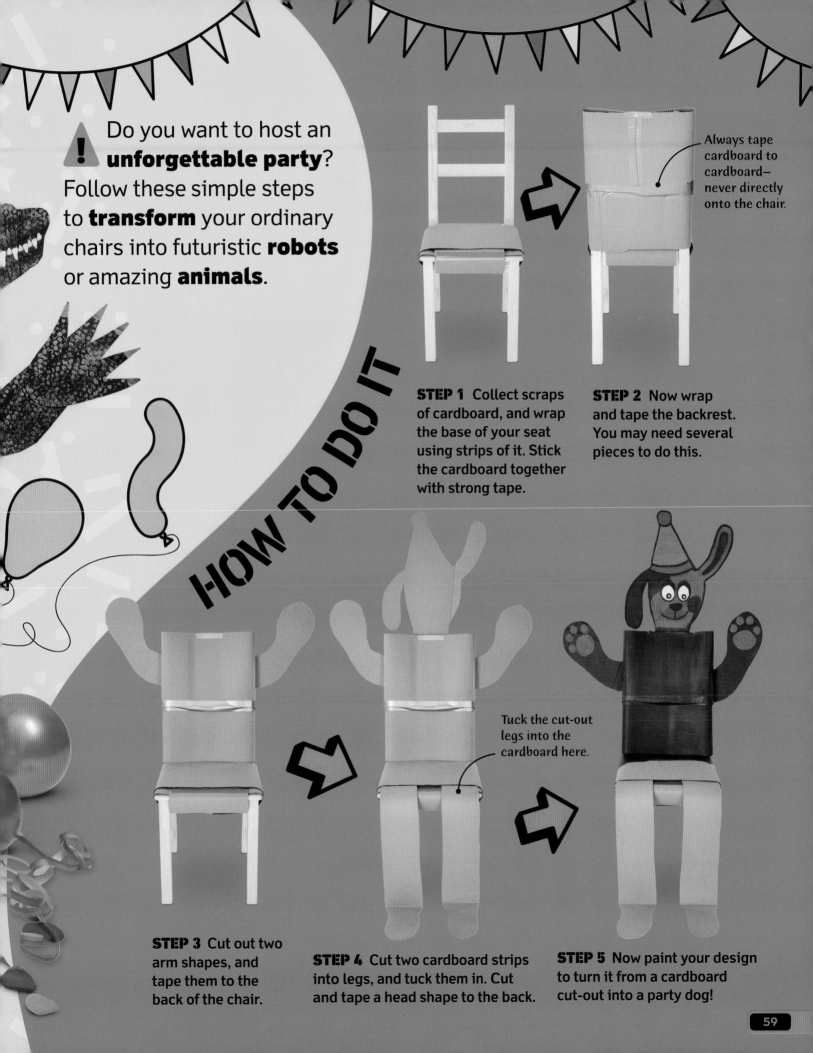

HOW TO DO IT

Always tape cardboard to cardboard— never directly onto the chair.

STEP 1 Collect scraps of cardboard, and wrap the base of your seat using strips of it. Stick the cardboard together with strong tape.

STEP 2 Now wrap and tape the backrest. You may need several pieces to do this.

STEP 3 Cut out two arm shapes, and tape them to the back of the chair.

STEP 4 Cut two cardboard strips into legs, and tuck them in. Cut and tape a head shape to the back.

Tuck the cut-out legs into the cardboard here.

STEP 5 Now paint your design to turn it from a cardboard cut-out into a party dog!

Being a **spy** is about remaining unseen while figuring out **clues** and gathering **top secret** information. These activities will help turn you into the next James Bond...

84 Write a spy code

Spies need to be able to communicate with each other in secret. One way they do this is with spy codes. They're good for planning where to have super secret spy meetings.

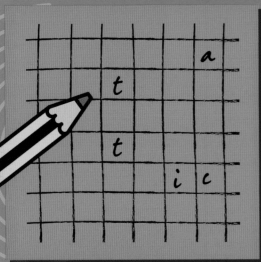

STEP 1 Draw a grid on a piece of paper. Write the location of your spy meeting on random squares. Then fill in the remaining squares with other letters.

STEP 2 Now get a second piece of paper the same size and carefully cut holes out of it in the same place as the letters that spell out the spy meeting place. This is your key.

TOP TIP
Use a sharp pencil to make a hole in the paper before using your scissors.

STEP 3 Leave the first piece of paper in your friend's room. Now you need to give them the key without anyone realizing.

85 Make a disguise

Great spies blend into crowds with the help of disguises. Practice wearing wigs, fake moustaches, hats, and sunglasses. Will your friends recognize you?

86 Keep a spy file

The best spies keep good notes. Write down anything that seems suspicious to you, draw maps, and take photos of things that could be used as evidence.

87 Take fingerprints

Think you've found the culprit but need more evidence? Dust their fingers with flour and then place some sticky tape over the finger. Peel it off to reveal their fingerprints! Now see if you can spot the same fingerprints at the scene of the crime.

DID YOU KNOW?
Every person's fingerprints are completely unique to them!

STEP 4 By placing the key on top of the first piece of paper, your friend will find out where they need to meet you!

MAKE SLIME

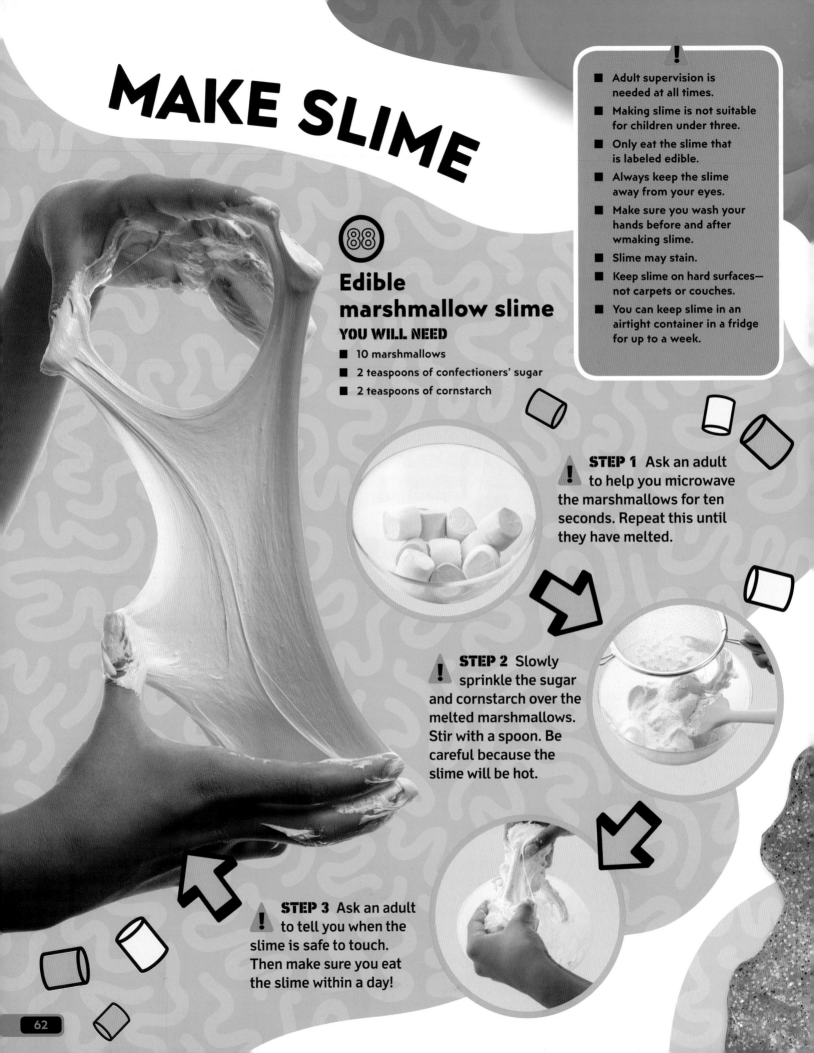

88

Edible marshmallow slime

YOU WILL NEED

- 10 marshmallows
- 2 teaspoons of confectioners' sugar
- 2 teaspoons of cornstarch

!
- Adult supervision is needed at all times.
- Making slime is not suitable for children under three.
- Only eat the slime that is labeled edible.
- Always keep the slime away from your eyes.
- Make sure you wash your hands before and after wmaking slime.
- Slime may stain.
- Keep slime on hard surfaces—not carpets or couches.
- You can keep slime in an airtight container in a fridge for up to a week.

! STEP 1 Ask an adult to help you microwave the marshmallows for ten seconds. Repeat this until they have melted.

! STEP 2 Slowly sprinkle the sugar and cornstarch over the melted marshmallows. Stir with a spoon. Be careful because the slime will be hot.

! STEP 3 Ask an adult to tell you when the slime is safe to touch. Then make sure you eat the slime within a day!

62

Glow-in-the-dark slime

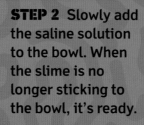

89

YOU WILL NEED
- ½ teaspoon of baking soda
- ½ cup (120 ml) of warm water
- ⅔ cup (140 ml) of clear craft glue
- Glow-in-the-dark poster paint
- Saline solution—it must contain boric acid or sodium borate

STEP 1 Add the baking soda, water, glue, and plenty of poster paint into a bowl.

STEP 2 Slowly add the saline solution to the bowl. When the slime is no longer sticking to the bowl, it's ready.

STEP 3 Turn off the lights, and watch it glow!

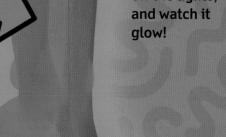

Glitter slime

90

YOU WILL NEED
- 3 tablespoons (45 ml) of peel-off face mask— they must contain polyvinyl alcohol
- Glitter
- 1 teaspoon of baking soda
- Saline solution—it must contain boric acid or sodium borate

STEP 1 Empty the face mask mixture into a bowl, and add the glitter to it.

STEP 3 Add the saline solution bit by bit and mix until the sparkly slime forms. Get stretching!

STEP 2 Mix in the baking soda.

91 Hangman

STEP 1 One player in a group chooses a word or phrase for the other players to guess. The first player underlines a blank space for each letter in the word or phrase.

STEP 2 The other players take turns guessing the letters.

STEP 3 If a letter is guessed correctly, the first player fills in a blank. If it is wrong, they draw part of the hangman.

STEP 4 The first player wins if the hangman is drawn before the word or phrase is guessed correctly.

Draw the post first, followed by the head, body, an arm, another arm, a leg, another leg, and finally the rope.

If there are two or more of the same letter in the word or phrase, fill them in when someone guesses the letter.

Write down any incorrect letters to the side of the hangman.

DRAWING GAMES

You won't **believe** how many different things you can do with a **pen** and **paper**! Challenge some of your friends to these drawing games, and see who comes out **on top**.

92 Beetle

Players take turns rolling a die. The number that a player rolls controls which part of a beetle they can draw. Each player must first roll a 6 to draw the body. The first whole beetle wins.

Rolling a 1 lets you draw an eye. You need to roll 1 twice to draw both eyes.

Rolling a 2 lets you draw an antenna. You must roll 2 twice to draw both antennae.

Rolling a 4 lets you draw a wing. You must roll 4 twice to draw both wings.

Rolling a 5 lets you draw the head. You must draw the head before you can add the eyes and antennae.

Rolling a 6 lets you draw the body. You need to draw the body before you can draw the other parts.

Rolling a 3 lets you draw a leg. You must roll 3 six times to draw six legs.

93 Tic-tac-toe

Two players draw a grid three squares tall and wide. They decide who will be "O" and who will be "X." The first player draws their symbol in an empty square. Then the second player does the same with theirs. The players take turns until a player wins with three in a row.

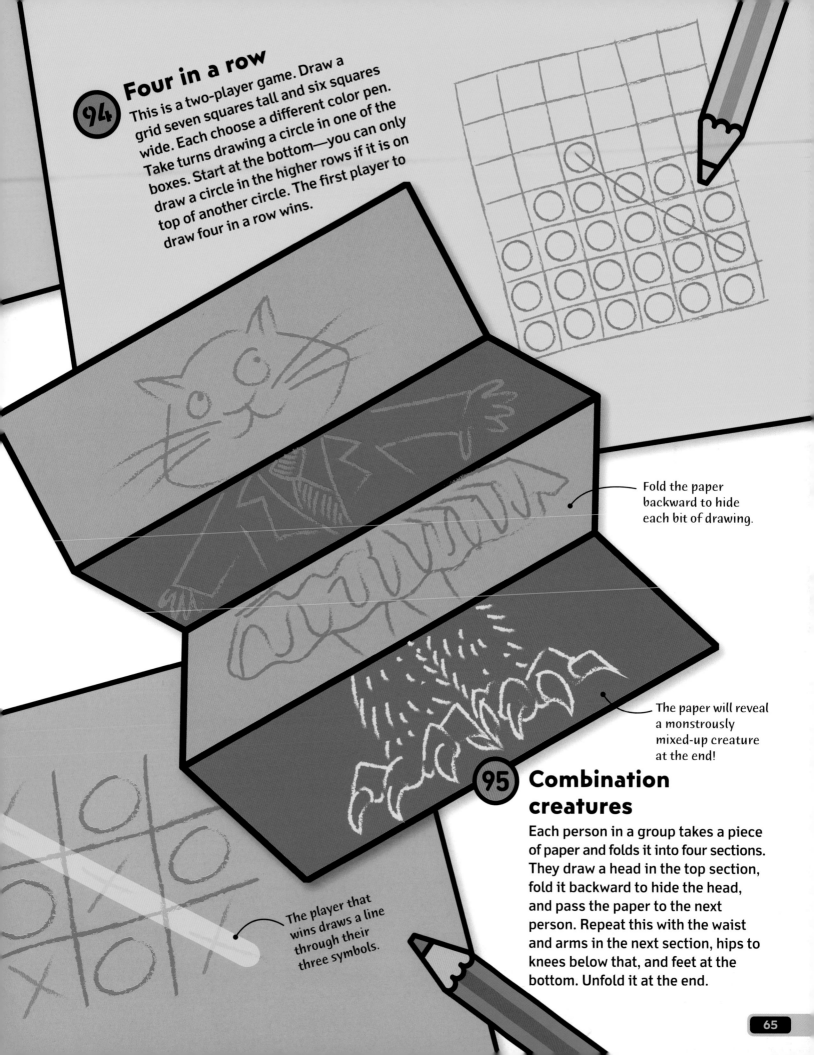

94 Four in a row

This is a two-player game. Draw a grid seven squares tall and six squares wide. Each choose a different color pen. Take turns drawing a circle in one of the boxes. Start at the bottom—you can only draw a circle in the higher rows if it is on top of another circle. The first player to draw four in a row wins.

Fold the paper backward to hide each bit of drawing.

The paper will reveal a monstrously mixed-up creature at the end!

95 Combination creatures

Each person in a group takes a piece of paper and folds it into four sections. They draw a head in the top section, fold it backward to hide the head, and pass the paper to the next person. Repeat this with the waist and arms in the next section, hips to knees below that, and feet at the bottom. Unfold it at the end.

The player that wins draws a line through their three symbols.

96 WRITE A SONG

Ever wanted to be a **songwriter**? Here we show you how. While there is no one set way to write a song, here are a few ideas to **get you started** on the road to singer-songwriter stardom!

Write the lyrics

First decide what your song is going to be about. It's often best to write about someone or something you know well—it might be about your best friend, your favorite sport, or your pet hamster! Then try writing the words, or lyrics, to the song.

Hum a tune

To help you find a tune, try humming a few notes out loud to see how they sound. Repeat different sounds until you get a tune you love.

VERSE 1

Songs are often broken into small sections of about four to six lines, called verses. It's great if you can make pairs of lines rhyme, but they don't have to.

CHORUS

The chorus of the song is repeated after each verse. It's best to make it nice and catchy and easy to sing, so save your best lines for the chorus.

The second verse should be different from the first verse. It should move the story on or discuss a related subject. You can have as many verses as you want!

VERSE 2

CHORUS

Repeat the chorus after the second verse, and so on until the end of the song. The song usually ends with the chorus.

Add instruments

Can you play any instruments? If so, you might want to play the instrument as backing for your song. Not all songs have lyrics, so you might want to create a tune with no words. This is called an instrumental.

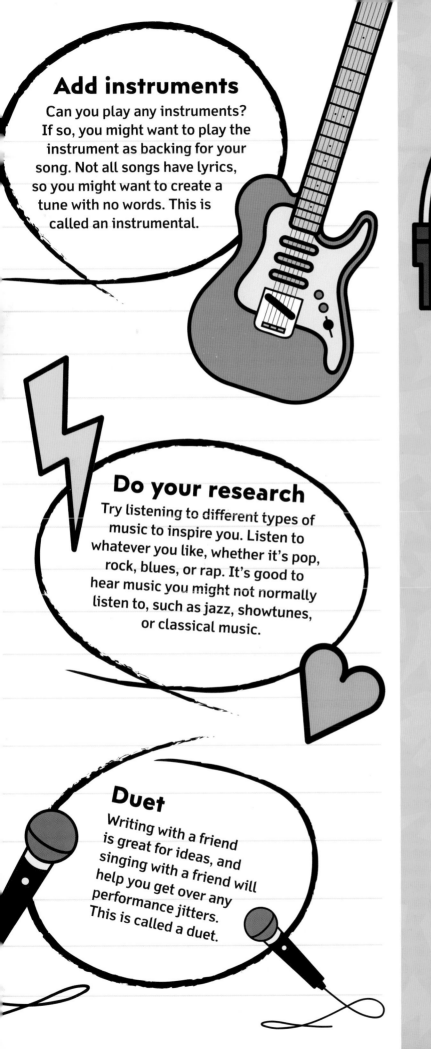

Do your research

Try listening to different types of music to inspire you. Listen to whatever you like, whether it's pop, rock, blues, or rap. It's good to hear music you might not normally listen to, such as jazz, showtunes, or classical music.

Duet

Writing with a friend is great for ideas, and singing with a friend will help you get over any performance jitters. This is called a duet.

97

Change a song

Pick one of your favorite songs, then change the words to make it funny or sad, or to make it about something completely different. Try changing the tune. How would a rap sound as a pop song?

98

Star performer

You can try recording yourself or do a live performance. Set up a "stage" at home. What props might you need? Choose your costume with care. Will you have background singers? Invite friends and family to watch!

99

Make a musical

Now you've written your song, why not try making a musical! This is a group of songs that connect together to make a story. Turn to pages 16–17 to learn how to add some dance moves.

MAKE YOUR OWN INSTRUMENT

You can make your own wind instrument with a few straws.

TOP TIP

Once you've made all three instruments, find two friends and form a band!

100

Rubber band guitar

Rock stars play guitars. Making an rubber band guitar may be your first step toward becoming a rock star.

STEP 2 Carefully cut a hole in the lid of a cardboard box. Put the plastic container inside the cardboard box, and decorate it. Rock on!

STEP 1 Find six rubber bands of different sizes. Line them up in order from narrowest to widest, then stretch them over a plastic container in order. Pluck them, and listen to how each one sounds different.

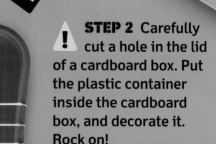

STEP 1 Grab a bunch of straws, and carefully cut them so that each one is ½ in (1 cm) shorter than the one before it.

STEP 2 Stick them together in height order using sticky tape. Then blow into the holes along the flat end.

MAKE NOISE!

What other items can you find that make noise? Try to invent your own instrument. What can you do to make it play different notes?

What sound is made by scrunching paper or foil?

(102)

Glass organ

With just a few glasses of water and a metal spoon, you can create your own organ! Fill each glass with a different amount of water, and gently tap them with the spoon.

Add food coloring to make the organ look cooler.

Does more water make the notes sound higher or lower?

103
Create a card
Fold a piece of heavy paper in half, and decorate it with drawings or a collage.

104
People chain
STEP 1 Fold a piece of paper over and over itself, like an accordion.

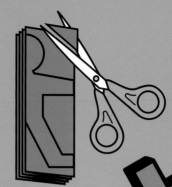

STEP 2 Draw half a person, and then cut around the edges. Make sure the arm goes all the way to the edge.

STEP 3 Now unfold your paper to reveal your perfect people chain!

THINGS TO DO WITH...

107
Name
Address line 1
Address line 2
Address line 3

Date

Write a letter
Why not send a letter to a friend instead of a text message? Put your name, address, and the date in the top-right corner, then start writing.

108
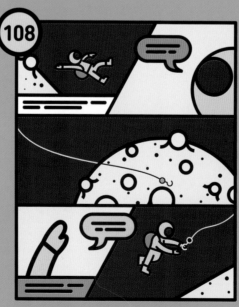

Comic
Divide your piece of paper into boxes and draw a comic story.

109
Make a fan
STEP 1 Fold a piece of paper over and over itself.

STEP 2 Pinch it with a clothespin at one end, and fan the rest of it out. Now decorate!

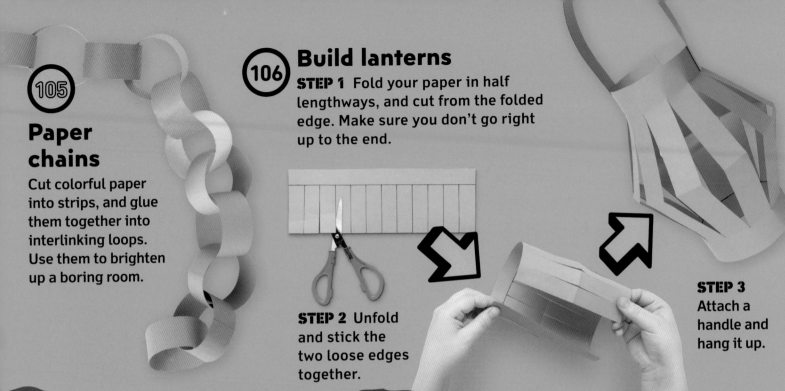

105 Paper chains

Cut colorful paper into strips, and glue them together into interlinking loops. Use them to brighten up a boring room.

106 Build lanterns

STEP 1 Fold your paper in half lengthways, and cut from the folded edge. Make sure you don't go right up to the end.

STEP 2 Unfold and stick the two loose edges together.

STEP 3 Attach a handle and hang it up.

A PIECE OF PAPER!

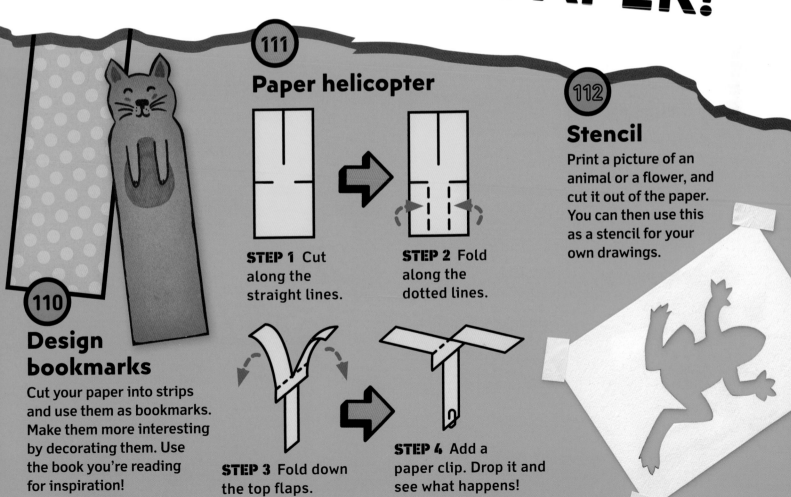

110 Design bookmarks

Cut your paper into strips and use them as bookmarks. Make them more interesting by decorating them. Use the book you're reading for inspiration!

111 Paper helicopter

STEP 1 Cut along the straight lines.

STEP 2 Fold along the dotted lines.

STEP 3 Fold down the top flaps.

STEP 4 Add a paper clip. Drop it and see what happens!

112 Stencil

Print a picture of an animal or a flower, and cut it out of the paper. You can then use this as a stencil for your own drawings.

71

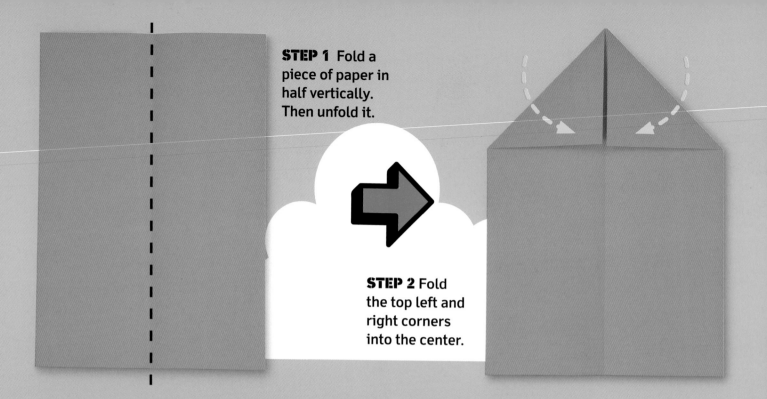

STEP 1 Fold a piece of paper in half vertically. Then unfold it.

STEP 2 Fold the top left and right corners into the center.

⑪⑬ MAKE A PAPER PLANE

With just a simple piece of **paper**, you can **conquer** the **skies**! How far can you make your paper plane **glide**?

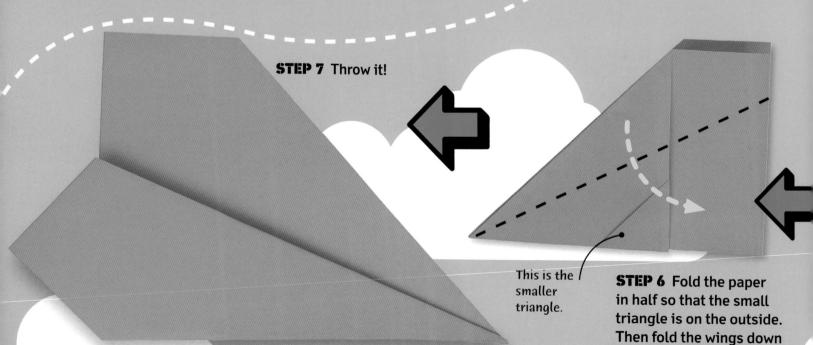

STEP 7 Throw it!

This is the smaller triangle.

STEP 6 Fold the paper in half so that the small triangle is on the outside. Then fold the wings down along the dotted line.

STEP 3 Fold the top triangle down so that it's about ½ in (1 cm) from the bottom. It should now look kind of like an envelope.

STEP 4 Fold the top left and right corners down so that they meet in the center.

STEP 5 Fold the smaller triangle up.

114

Paper plane darts

Make a simple dartboard out of construction paper. Take turns aiming for the bull's-eye.

PAPER PLANE FACTORY

Come up with new, inventive designs for other paper planes. You might find that some fly a lot faster or farther than others.

Try using different colored paper.

Don't forget to decorate your planes.

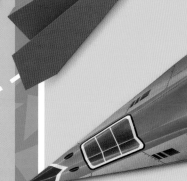

Always crease the folds well.

⚠️ **STEP 1** Cut a piece of paper into a square.

STEP 2 Fold the paper in half vertically and unfold it. Then fold it horizontally and unfold it again.

(115) MAKE A FORTUNE TELLER

Do you ever wish you could **predict** the **future**? Well, wish no further—a **fortune teller** does exactly that. Your friends won't believe their ears when you reveal their **destiny**.

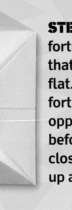

STEP 7 Open the fortune teller up so that it's completely flat. Write out your fortunes (see opposite page) before you close it back up again.

STEP 6 Using both of your hands, poke your thumbs and index fingers into the pockets on the outside. Bring your thumbs and fingers in toward each other, squeezing the two ends together. It should now look like four peaks.

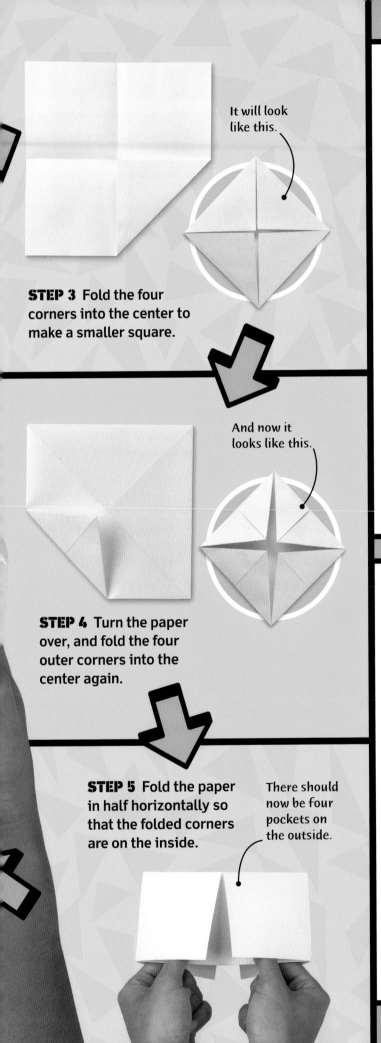

It will look like this.

STEP 3 Fold the four corners into the center to make a smaller square.

And now it looks like this.

STEP 4 Turn the paper over, and fold the four outer corners into the center again.

STEP 5 Fold the paper in half horizontally so that the folded corners are on the inside.

There should now be four pockets on the outside.

HOW TO FILL IN YOUR FORTUNE TELLER

Fill in the four corner squares with your chosen colors. The eight triangles next to the colored squares are where you write the numbers. The smaller, inner square, made up of eight segments, is where you write the answers to the questions.

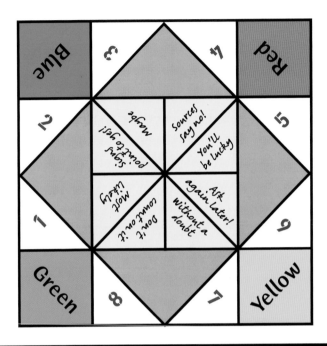

HOW TO READ SOMEONE'S FORTUNE

1: Tell your friend to ask a question about themselves that has a yes, no, or maybe answer.

2: Ask them to pick a color.

3: Move the fortune teller in and out the same number of times as the number of letters in that color.

4: Ask your friend to pick a number.

5: Move the fortune teller in and out that number of times.

6: Ask them to pick a number a second time.

7: Unfold the flap with that number on it to reveal the answer to their question.

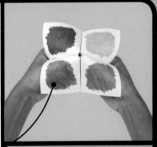

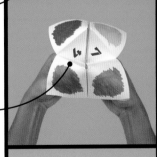

MAKE A PAPER FROG

STEP 1 Start off with a square piece of green origami paper. Fold it in half horizontally and then unfold it.

STEP 2 Next fold it in half vertically.

STEP 3 Fold the paper again vertically and then unfold it. You'll use these creases to guide you later.

STEP 8 Using the existing creases, fold the two edges in toward each other so they meet in the middle. The top of the square will then form a triangle as you fold it down.

STEP 9 Fold the bottom half of the paper up horizontally so that it touches the bottom of the triangle.

STEP 10 Fold the left side of the paper in half and tuck it behind the triangle. Do not fold the triangle.

STEP 15 Place your index fingers inside the flaps on either side of the rectangle. Pull the inner corners out and flatten the paper. It should now look like a boat.

STEP 16 Fold the left and right corners down so they meet in the middle.

STEP 17 Fold the bottom-right corner of the triangle up. Fold it at an angle, as shown in the image. Repeat on the left side.

STEP 4 Fold the top square in half diagonally and unfold it.

STEP 5 Repeat the previous step on the opposite side and unfold it again.

STEP 6 Turn your origami paper over.

STEP 7 Fold the top square in half horizontally. Unfold it and turn the paper over again.

STEP 11 Repeat the previous step on the right side.

STEP 12 Fold the bottom half of the paper up horizontally so that it touches the bottom of the triangle.

STEP 13 Fold the front of the left square in half diagonally. Crease it well and then unfold.

STEP 14 Repeat the previous step with the right square. Again, crease it well and unfold.

STEP 18 Fold the bottom-right part of the paper out. Fold it at an angle, as shown in the image. Repeat on the left side.

STEP 19 Fold the whole frog in half horizontally so the bottom comes up.

STEP 20 Fold half of the rectangle back horizontally. Make sure you crease this fold well.

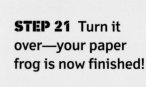

STEP 21 Turn it over—your paper frog is now finished!

Turn the page to find out how to make your frog hop!

Try to keep your frog in its lane. It's harder than you think!

(117)

Frog racing

Make a few frogs, then challenge your friends or family to a race. Set up start and finish lines and see who can be the first person to make their frog hop to victory!

START

Press down on the back of the frog and then let go to make it jump.

HOP IT!

The fun doesn't stop once your **frog** is finished. There are all sorts of **games** you could **play** with it. Here are a few ideas to get you started—it's time to perfect your **jumping** skills!

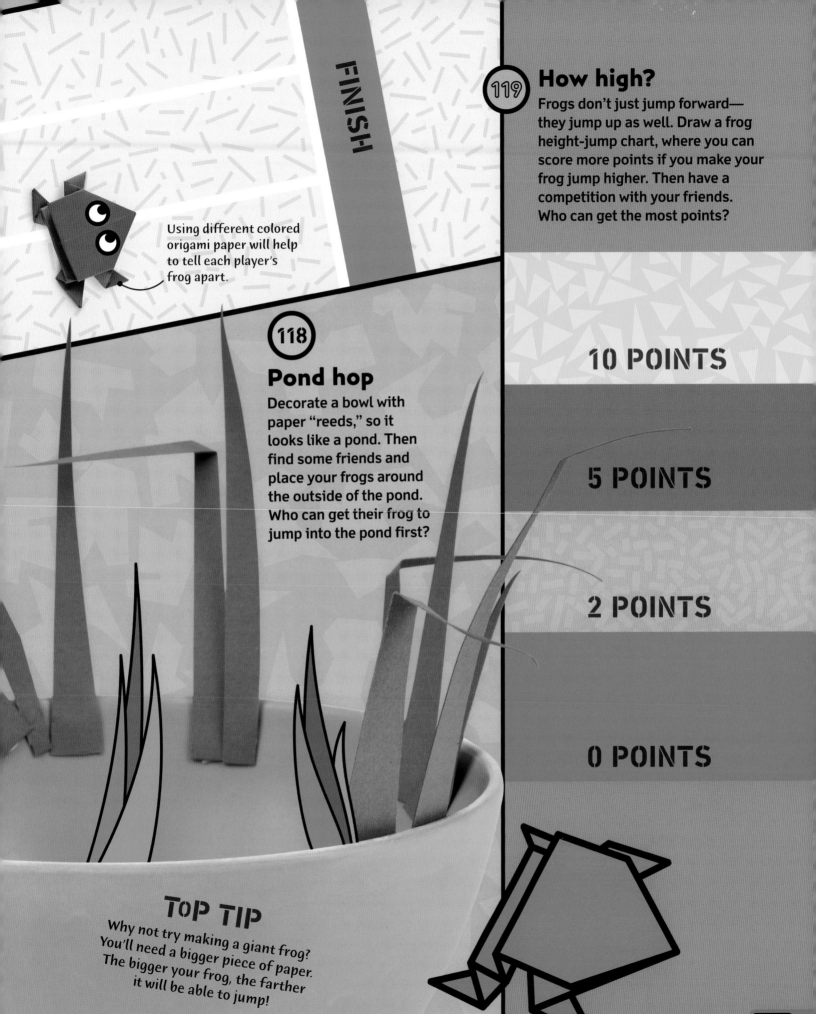

FINISH

Using different colored origami paper will help to tell each player's frog apart.

118

Pond hop

Decorate a bowl with paper "reeds," so it looks like a pond. Then find some friends and place your frogs around the outside of the pond. Who can get their frog to jump into the pond first?

119

How high?

Frogs don't just jump forward— they jump up as well. Draw a frog height-jump chart, where you can score more points if you make your frog jump higher. Then have a competition with your friends. Who can get the most points?

10 POINTS

5 POINTS

2 POINTS

0 POINTS

TOP TIP

Why not try making a giant frog? You'll need a bigger piece of paper. The bigger your frog, the farther it will be able to jump!

TEST YOUR FRIENDS

There are lots of different ways of creating fun **challenges** for your **friends**. All you need is **paper and a pen** to make your very own maze, quiz, riddle, or word search. Who will be the **champion** at the end of the day?

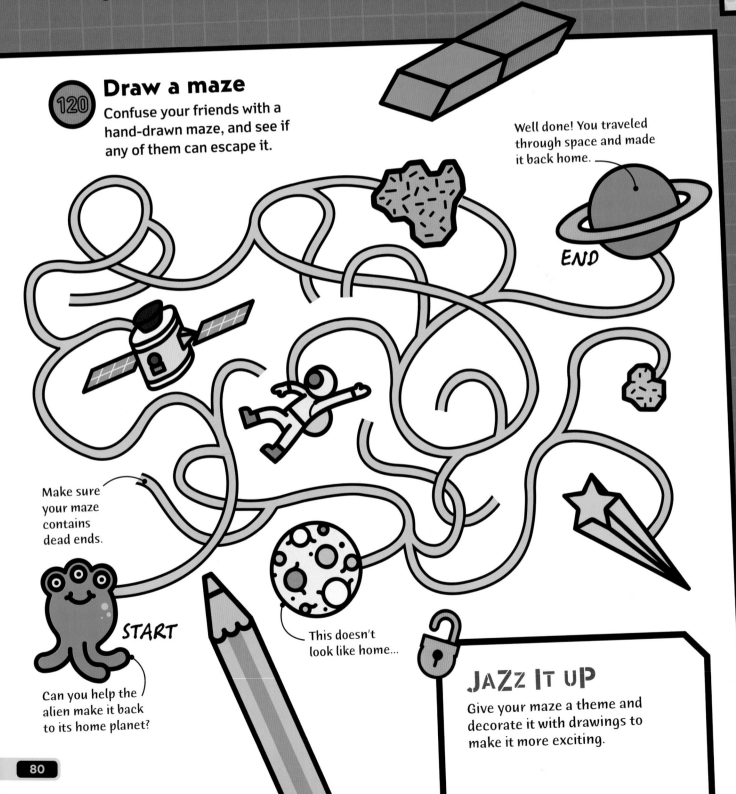

120 **Draw a maze**
Confuse your friends with a hand-drawn maze, and see if any of them can escape it.

Well done! You traveled through space and made it back home.

END

Make sure your maze contains dead ends.

START

Can you help the alien make it back to its home planet?

This doesn't look like home...

JAZZ IT UP
Give your maze a theme and decorate it with drawings to make it more exciting.

Cut up colorful paper to make your quiz cards.

121 Create a quiz

Find out who has the best general knowledge with a simple multiple choice quiz. Start by writing out ten questions on quiz cards. Then write four answers for each question and make sure only one of them is correct. Now let your friends battle it out to become quiz champion!

122 Try out a riddle

Are your friends as clever as they say they are? Test them with these riddles to see if you can get their brains in a twist. Then try to come up with your own. (The answers are at the bottom of the page.)

1. What gets wetter the more it dries?

2. My one-story home has yellow walls, a yellow chair, a yellow telephone, and a yellow dog. What color are the stairs?

3. I'm as light as a feather, but even the strongest person can't hold me for more than a couple of minutes. What am I?

4. What has two hands and a face but no arms and legs?

123 MAKE A WORD SEARCH

See how good your friends are at spotting hidden words in a homemade word search.

STEP 1 Draw a grid with ten columns and ten rows. You should have 100 squares in total.

STEP 2 Fill in the empty squares with eight words. Each square should contain only one letter. The words can be horizontal, vertical, or diagonal.

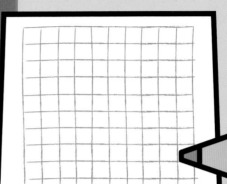

space
asteroid
moon
astronaut
star
rocket
alien
planet

STEP 3 Write down your words next to the side of the word search so that your friends know what to look for.

STEP 4 Fill in the remaining squares with random letters to disguise your words.

Riddle answers: 1. A towel. 2. There are no stairs in a one-story home! 3. Breath 4. A clock.

81

GO GREEN!

People create lots of **garbage** that is bad for the **environment** and hard to get rid of. Here are some ideas to help you do your bit for the planet. **Reduce, reuse, recycle!**

REDUCE
The best way to not waste things is to not buy them in the first place.

REUSE
Try to find ways to use things again, instead of throwing them away.

RECYCLE
Recycling means taking old things and turning them into something totally new.

124

Reusing cards
Plenty of things can be reused before you recycle them. Try making gift tags from old birthday or holiday cards.

⚠ STEP 1 Cut out your favorite picture or pattern from the card.

STEP 2 Make a hole in the picture using a hole punch.

STEP 3 Thread a piece of string through the hole. Your gift tag is ready to go!

You can use some types of garbage to make compost, which helps plants grow. Start with a compost bin, add some soil, then follow this recipe. Stir occasionally, and your compost should be ready to spread around plants in about a month.

Two parts scrap paper

Shredded newspaper and office paper

Egg cartons and used cardboard

One part green waste

Vegetable peelings

Coffee grounds

Grass cuttings

Tea leaves from used tea bags

125 MAKE COMPOST

TOP TIP

Not all food makes good compost. Here are some things you should keep out of your compost mix.

Chilli peppers

Garlic

Citrus fruit

Meat

Fish

Dairy

Eggs

126 Swap shop

Organize a swap game with your friends to get "new" stuff for free! Go through your things and pick out anything you don't want anymore. Make sure your parents don't mind you getting rid of it. Ask your friends to do the same, then meet up and trade!

127 Clean up outside

⚠️ If you see litter out and about, ask an adult if it's safe to pick up, then throw it away! You'll need gloves for this. Sort paper, plastics, and bottles into recycling bins, just as you would at home. How much trash can you collect?

RECYCLED ANIMALS

Try turning **trash** into **art** with these fun **craft** ideas. They all feature something you might usually **throw away**. Which will you make first?

TOP TIP

Use the bottom of the bottle from the bee hotel (see pages 102–103) to make your turtle.

Use glue to stick the flaps down once you've folded them.

(128) Plate penguin

STEP 1 Fold two sides of a paper plate in toward the middle, then fold the top down over them. These folds will be the penguin's wings and head.

(129) Bottle-top beetles

STEP 1 Paint your bottle-top to look like a beetle's body. Ladybugs work well.

(130) ⚠ Bottle turtle

STEP 1 Cut this shape from a piece of thick paper or cardboard. The body should be the same size as the bottom of a plastic bottle.

STEP 2 Carefully cut the bottom off a green plastic bottle, then stick it in the center of your turtle shape with glue or tape.

STEP 3 Stick googly eyes onto your penguin's face. Cut its beak and feet from orange paper, then stick them on. Your penguin is complete!

STEP 2 Paint the penguin's head and wings black, leaving its tummy white.

STEP 2 Flip the bottle-top over, and fill it with modeling clay. Stick in pipe cleaners to make your beetle's legs.

STEP 3 Make some more beetles to keep yours company!

Use different colors and patterns to make other beetles.

STEP 3 Draw eyes on your turtle, then use felt-tip pens to decorate its face, flippers, and tail.

DID YOU KNOW?
Sea turtles can live more than 80 years!

STEP 1 Wash and dry your carton, then cut a semicircle out of its two sides. Don't cut along the straight edge of the shape— you want to make flaps, not holes.

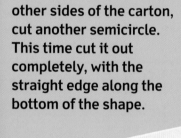

YOU WILL NEED

- Milk or juice carton
- Scissors
- Cardboard and paint for decoration
- Straw
- Bird seed
- String

STEP 2 From one of the other sides of the carton, cut another semicircle. This time cut it out completely, with the straight edge along the bottom of the shape.

(131) FEED THE BIRDS

! **Birds** are everywhere! If you'd like to see some a **little closer** than usual, try leaving some **food** out for them. This snazzy bird feeder is a colorful way to feed your **feathered friends**.

STEP 3 Decorate your carton to look like the bird of your choice. The flaps are wings, and you can add a cardboard beak to make it more realistic.

Poke a pencil through the carton under the main hole. It needs to go all the way through to create a small hole on both sides.

Attach your bird feeder to a branch with some string.

TOP TIP

Different types of food will attract different birds. If you don't have any bird seed, you could try leaving out some fruits, nuts, or even worms!

(132)

Make a bird calendar

Take a look out your window. You'll see different birds at different times of the year. Try keeping a bird calendar to see which birds visit your home during which months.

STEP 4 Push a straw into the hole you just made, and put some bird seed in the bottom of the carton.

The straw becomes a handy perch for visiting birds to sit on.

May 14   May 15

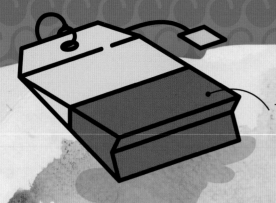

To make your map look old, press a wet tea bag against the edges to color it like parchment. You can try crumpling up the paper a bit, too.

Palm trees could stand for plants or lamps.

STEP 1 Draw your island map on a big sheet of paper. Each feature should relate to an item in the room—for example, a rug might be a lake, and a bookcase a waterfall.

STEP 2 Decide what your treasure will be, and then hide it in your chosen location. Figure out where it is on the map, and then draw a big red X to mark the spot!

STEP 3 It's now time to play the game. Show your friends the map, and see if they can find the hidden treasure!

Draw each item in the same position as the object it represents—so if your rug is in the center of the room, put the lake in the center of your drawing.

A boulder could be your TV.

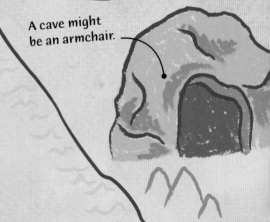

(133) TREASURE HUNT

A cave might be an armchair.

Make your own treasure hunt game! First decide where the **hunt** will take place. It's best if it's somewhere you know well, such as in a room in your home. Then draw your very own **treasure island map**.

A waterfall could
be a bookcase.

Your brown couch
could become a
shipwreck.

You might draw
a bear instead of
your pet dog!

134 Make a treasure chest

Find an old box—it might be a shoe box
or something smaller. Decorate it to look
like a pirate's chest,
then fill it with
goodies, such as
candy, small
toys, or coins.

135 Bury a time capsule

A time capsule is a container full of things
from the present, such as photos, books,
and toys. Hide the capsule away in your
yard or in a cupboard, for your future self
(or someone else) to find in years to come!

If hiding your capsule outside,
you'll need a tough container, such
as a steel box. If it's going to be
inside, a shoe box will do!

DID YOU KNOW?

Time capsules were sent into space
on two Voyager spacecraft in 1977.
They held recordings of sounds
and pictures from Earth. The
recordings were sent to tell
any possible alien life-forms
what life on Earth is like.

MAP IT OUT

Sick of **getting lost**? Sounds like you need to make a map! You can do so with graph paper and colored pencils. Decide **what you want the map to show**—it could be your backyard, your neighborhood, or even a whole city. Use the **squares** to plot where everything goes.

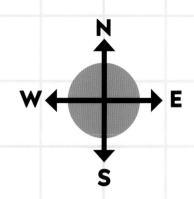

Which way?

Add a compass, such as this one, so that you can see which direction things are facing—whether North (N), South (S), East (E), or West (W).

Make a key

Think about what you want to show on the map. Make a list, and then do simple drawings for each one. This is your key for the map. Here are the type of things you may want to show:

House

Park

Trees

Water

Candy store

Pet shop

Grocery store

Playground

Bridge

Road

School

This is a row of stores.

The outline of the store stays the same, and the picture inside tells you what type it is.

Keep your key pictures simple—you might have to draw a lot of them!

Use broken lines to show roads.

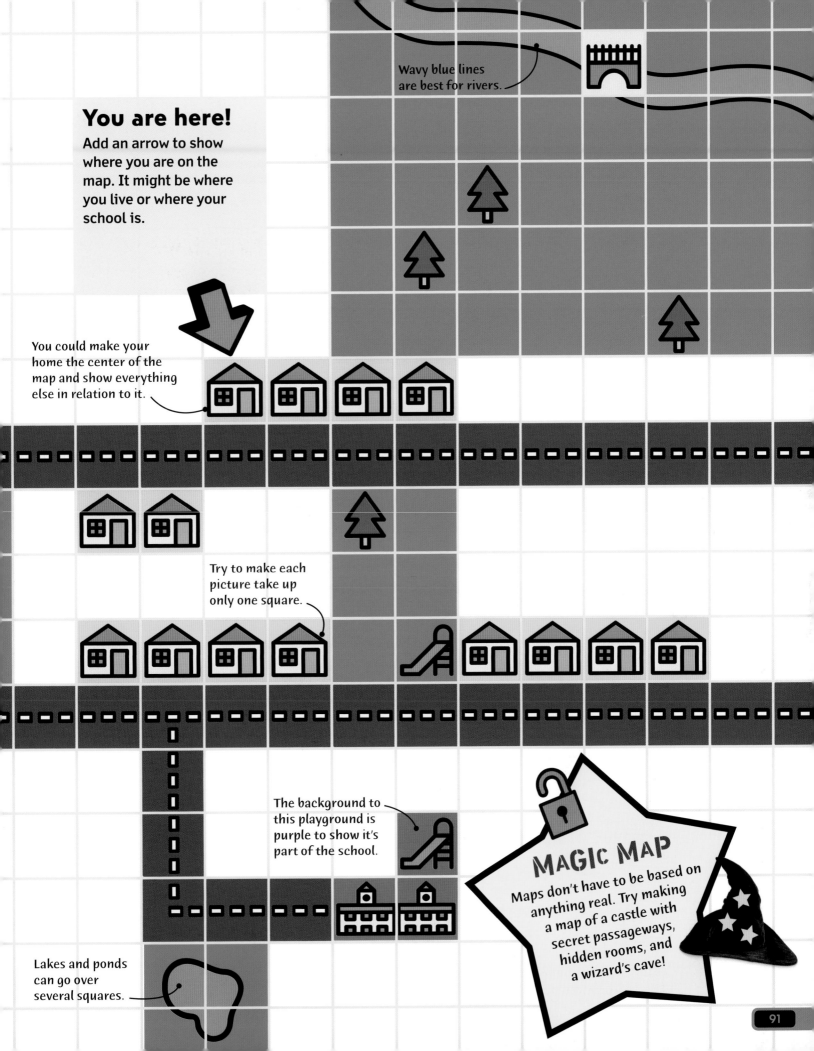

You are here!

Add an arrow to show where you are on the map. It might be where you live or where your school is.

Wavy blue lines are best for rivers.

You could make your home the center of the map and show everything else in relation to it.

Try to make each picture take up only one square.

The background to this playground is purple to show it's part of the school.

Lakes and ponds can go over several squares.

MAGIC MAP

Maps don't have to be based on anything real. Try making a map of a castle with secret passageways, hidden rooms, and a wizard's cave!

PRINTING

You can print all sorts of **patterns and designs** using everyday items. All you have to do is cover your chosen item in **paint**, press it onto **paper**, and slowly lift it off to uncover what you've left behind!

139 Fruits and vegetables

Although it may not look like it, fruits and vegetables can produce great prints. Cut bell peppers and lemons in half, and use celery sticks to print amazing flowers.

138 Bubble wrap

Try cutting shapes out of bubble wrap to make cool patterns.

137 Leaf prints

Leaves can create really beautiful prints. Collect lots of different types, paint them in different colors, and print them onto paper!

Styrofoam printing

Sometimes you might want to print the same image several times. Styrofoam lets you make identical prints, making them perfect for cards or posters.

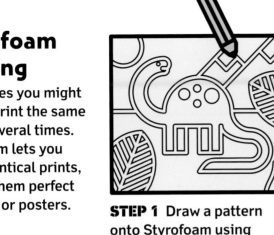

STEP 1 Draw a pattern onto Styrofoam using a pencil. Make sure you press down hard.

STEP 2 Paint over the top of your tile using a paint roller, so that the surface is evenly coated.

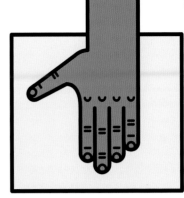

STEP 3 Press the painted Styrofoam onto a piece of plain paper.

STEP 4 Carefully lift off the tile to reveal your print! Now repeat as many times as you like.

Frisbee bowling

STEP 1 Line up ten plastic bottles in a triangle formation.

STEP 2 Take turns throwing the Frisbee at the bottles. Try to knock down as many as you can. Each player gets two attempts.

STEP 3 Record how many bottles each player knocks down per round, and repeat for ten rounds.

STEP 4 Add up the scores at the end to see who is the champion Frisbee bowler!

DID YOU KNOW?
Before the modern-day Frisbee was created, people used to throw pie pans!

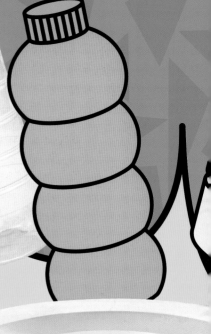

FRISBEE GAMES

Who knew **throwing a disk** through the air could be so **fun**? There are so many things you can do with a **Frisbee**—here are just a few **games** to get you started (all of them must be played outdoors).

142 Frisbee golf

Frisbee golf follows the same rules as golf. Players must land their Frisbee in different numbered "holes"—in this case, chained baskets—in the least number of throws. You can re-create this game at home using laundry baskets or plastic buckets. The player with the lowest score at the end of the game wins.

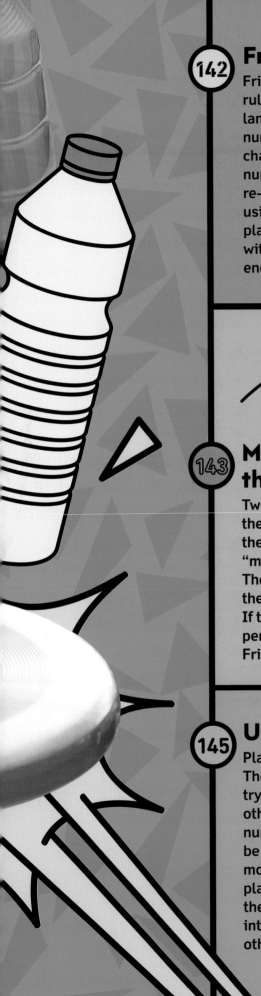

143 Monkey in the middle

Two people throw the Frisbee between themselves. One person, the "monkey," stands in the middle. The monkey has to try to intercept the Frisbee while it's being thrown. If they catch the Frisbee, the person who has just thrown the Frisbee becomes the new monkey.

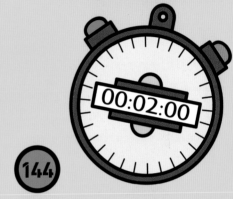

144 Throwing race

Form teams of two, and have partners stand around 3 ft (1 m) away from each other. See how many times you can throw the Frisbee to each other in two minutes. Highest score wins.

145 Ultimate Frisbee

Players are split into two teams. The aim of Ultimate Frisbee is to try to get the Frisbee into the other team's end zone the most number of times. The Frisbee can be thrown between teammates to move it up and down the field, but players must stop moving when they catch it. The Frisbee can be intercepted, or caught by the other team, at any point.

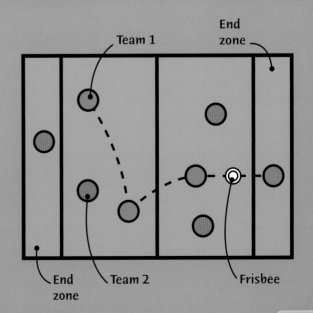

End zone

Team 1

End zone

End zone

Team 2

Frisbee

146 CREATE YOUR OWN SPORTS EVENT

What better way to spend a **whole day** than by running your own **sports event**? Have any of your friends and family been hiding a **secret athletic talent**? There's only one way to find out…

Create a schedule

Every sports event needs a schedule. What will you include in yours? Here are some ideas, but don't feel like you have to stick to them!

Time	Event
11:30	Opening ceremony
12:00	Triple jump
1:00	Synchronized dancing
2:30	Long jump
3:00	Shotput with a tennis ball
4:00	Cartwheel competition
4:30	Egg and spoon race
5:00	Wheelbarrow race

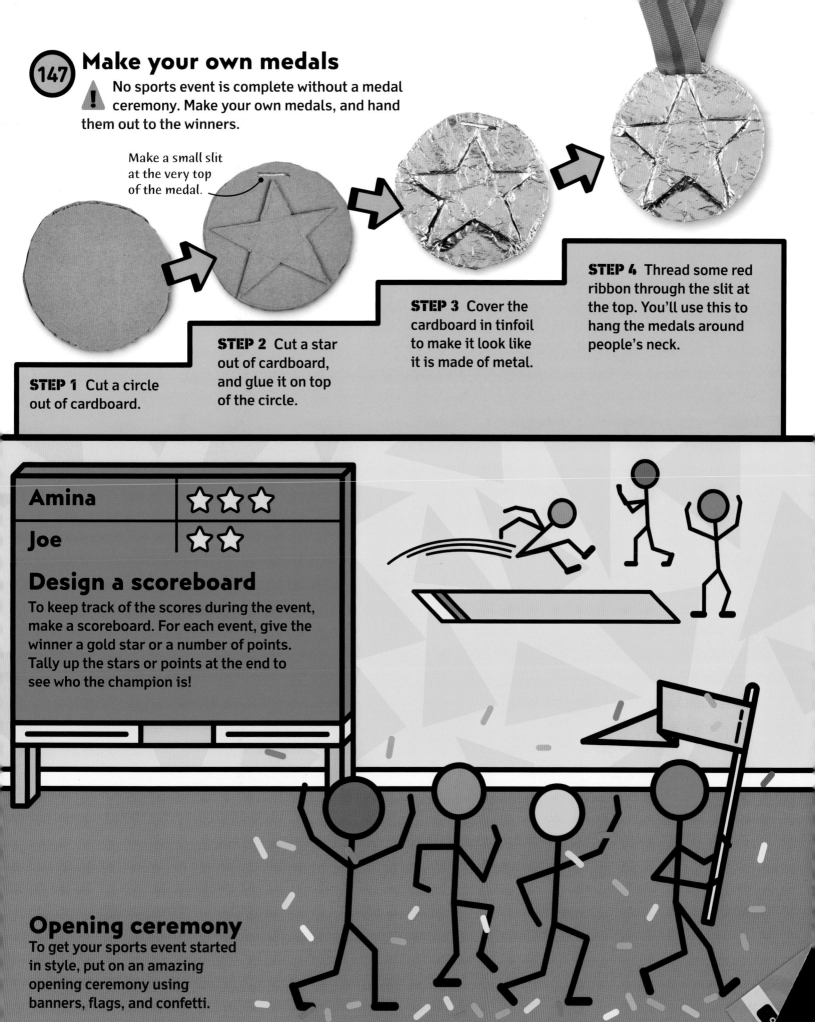

147 Make your own medals

⚠️ No sports event is complete without a medal ceremony. Make your own medals, and hand them out to the winners.

Make a small slit at the very top of the medal.

STEP 1 Cut a circle out of cardboard.

STEP 2 Cut a star out of cardboard, and glue it on top of the circle.

STEP 3 Cover the cardboard in tinfoil to make it look like it is made of metal.

STEP 4 Thread some red ribbon through the slit at the top. You'll use this to hang the medals around people's neck.

Amina	⭐⭐⭐
Joe	⭐⭐

Design a scoreboard

To keep track of the scores during the event, make a scoreboard. For each event, give the winner a gold star or a number of points. Tally up the stars or points at the end to see who the champion is!

Opening ceremony

To get your sports event started in style, put on an amazing opening ceremony using banners, flags, and confetti.

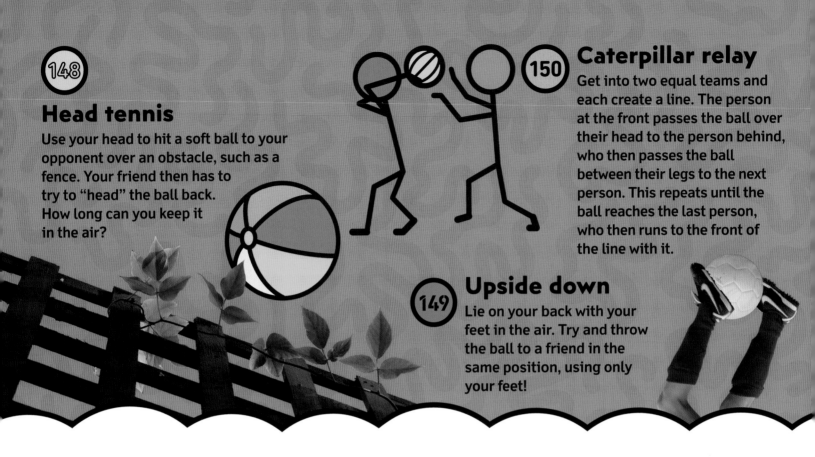

(148) Head tennis

Use your head to hit a soft ball to your opponent over an obstacle, such as a fence. Your friend then has to try to "head" the ball back. How long can you keep it in the air?

(150) Caterpillar relay

Get into two equal teams and each create a line. The person at the front passes the ball over their head to the person behind, who then passes the ball between their legs to the next person. This repeats until the ball reaches the last person, who then runs to the front of the line with it.

(149) Upside down

Lie on your back with your feet in the air. Try and throw the ball to a friend in the same position, using only your feet!

THINGS TO DO WITH...

(153) Keepy uppy

See who can keep a ball in the air the longest. You can use any part of your body, such as your feet, chest, and head, but not your hands.

(154) Bucket game

Gather some large buckets, and label each one with a different number of points. Place the bigger numbers farther away and the smaller numbers close to you. Then attempt to throw a ball into the buckets. The person who scores the most points after five turns is the winner.

50

100

20

10

5

151
Bocce

⚠️ Bocce is a popular game in France, where it is known as "boules." You take turns tossing balls as close as possible to a smaller ball called a jack. The person who throws their ball the closest to the jack is the winner.

152
Balance it
Try balancing a ball on your head. How long can you keep it there? Can you walk around without it falling off? Can you spin the ball on your finger?

A BALL!

155
Soccer golf
The idea of this game is to kick a soccer ball onto a target using as few shots as possible. Use tree trunks or stumps as targets. Make sure everyone takes their first shot from the same place.

156
Blanket catch
Stretch out a small blanket and use it to launch a ball to another player, who has to catch it in their own blanket. You can also play in pairs, with one person at either end of each blanket.

157
Funny walk
Squeeze a large, soft ball between your knees and try walking around without dropping it. This isn't as easy as it looks!

Orion

This is one of the best-known constellations. It shows a hunter, with three stars in a row making up his belt.

The Great Bear

The Great Bear is also known as "Ursa Major." It has a bright star called Mizar in its tail.

NORTHERN STARS

These constellations can be seen from the top half of the Earth—the "northern hemisphere."

158

GO STARGAZING

The stars in the night sky can be linked up into **patterns** called **constellations**. You can see different constellations depending on where you are in the world and what time of year it is. Head outside and go **star hunting**!

SOUTHERN STARS

These constellations can be seen from the bottom half of the Earth—the "southern hemisphere."

Centaur

A centaur is half-man and half-horse. Centaurs appear in ancient Greek stories.

Dog

Also called "Canis Major," the dog is home to Sirius, the brightest star in the sky.

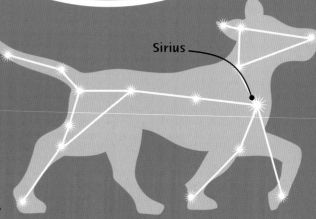

Sirius

The Dragon

The Dragon is also called "Draco." Its brightest star is in the dragon's head.

159 Keep a moon journal

Try sketching the moon each night. You should be able to see it changing.

New moon

Waxing crescent

First quarter

Waxing gibbous

Full moon

Waning gibbous

Last quarter

Waning crescent

New moon

The moon moves around the Earth once a month. As it travels, it appears to change shape. This is because the sun lights up different amounts of the moon's surface as the moon moves. The different shapes we see are called moon phases.

The Southern Cross

This is the smallest constellation in the sky, but its simple shape makes it easy to spot.

160 Look for a meteor shower

Meteors are shooting stars—particles of dust that leave behind trails of light as they burn up when they enter Earth's atmosphere. Many meteor showers happen at the same time each year. See if you can spot one!

Name of shower	Time of year	Where in the world
Lyrids	April 22-26	Northern hemisphere
Eta Aquarids	May 6	Southern hemisphere
Perseids	August 11-13	Both
Geminids	December 13-15	Both

Each meteor has a streak of light running along behind it.

NATURE DETECTIVE

The natural world is filled with **fascinating** creatures. Investigate and discover the secrets these **animals** have to tell!

162 Bird-spotting

Did you know birds are the modern descendants of dinosaurs? Grab a pair of binoculars, and make a list of all the kinds of birds you see.

STEP 2
Get an adult to trim the bamboo stems so that they are the same length as the cut-out part of the bottle.

STEP 1 Carefully cut off both ends of a plastic drink bottle.

161

MAKE A BEE HOTEL

⚠ Give the bees in your yard or a local park a cozy place to stay. You will need an adult's help for parts of this project.

YOU WILL NEED
- One 2-liter plastic drink bottle
- Scissors
- Enough bamboo stems to fill the bottle
- Twine

163

Bug collecting

Inspect bugs up close by collecting them and placing them in an empty jar. Cover the top with paper towel, and secure it onto the jar with a rubber band. Make sure you poke air holes in the top of the paper towel, and don't keep your bugs in there for too long!

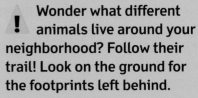

164

Look for animal tracks

 Wonder what different animals live around your neighborhood? Follow their trail! Look on the ground for the footprints left behind.

DiD YOU KNOW?

Bees will only sting you if you disturb them—and only female bees have a stinger.

STEP 4
Tie two pieces of twine tightly around the bottle to keep it all together.

STEP 5 Thread another piece of twine loosely around the other pieces of twine, and tie it with a knot. Now your bee hotel is ready to be hung! Find a tree or fence outdoors where you can hang the hotel about 3 ft (1 m) above the ground. Soon it will be *buzzing* with activity.

STEP 3 Fill the bottle with bamboo stems. Bee hotels work best when the bamboo holes are different sizes.

(165) POM-POMS

These **fluffy decorations** come in all **colors** and **sizes** and are quick to make. Yarn, paper or cardboard, and scissors are the only things you need to start creating a **handmade pom-pom**, so what are you waiting for?

⚠ STEP 3 When you've finished wrapping the disks, tuck the end of the yarn under some of the other yarn. Use a pair of scissors to cut through the yarn around the outside of the two disks. Make sure you cut the whole way around.

Wrap the yarn around and around your paper donuts.

⚠ STEP 1 Draw a 3-in (8-cm) wide circle on cardboard or thick paper. Cut it out, and draw a 1-in (2.5-cm) wide circle in the center of the larger circle. Cut out the smaller circle. Repeat this step to make two donut-shaped pieces.

STEP 2 Once you've made your disks, hold them together and start wrapping your yarn around them. Use four strands of yarn at once to make the pom-pom thick. Make sure you tuck your first strand under a later one to hold it in place.

---

(166)

Pom-pom wreath

Once you've made a bunch of pom-poms, what's next? A pom-pom wreath is simple to create and will brighten up any room.

Use the loose yarn from the pom-pom to tie it tightly to the hanger.

STEP 2 Cover the entire wreath in pom-poms. Don't leave any space between them.

 STEP 1 Stretch a wire coat hanger into a circle, and start attaching your pre-made pom-poms onto it.

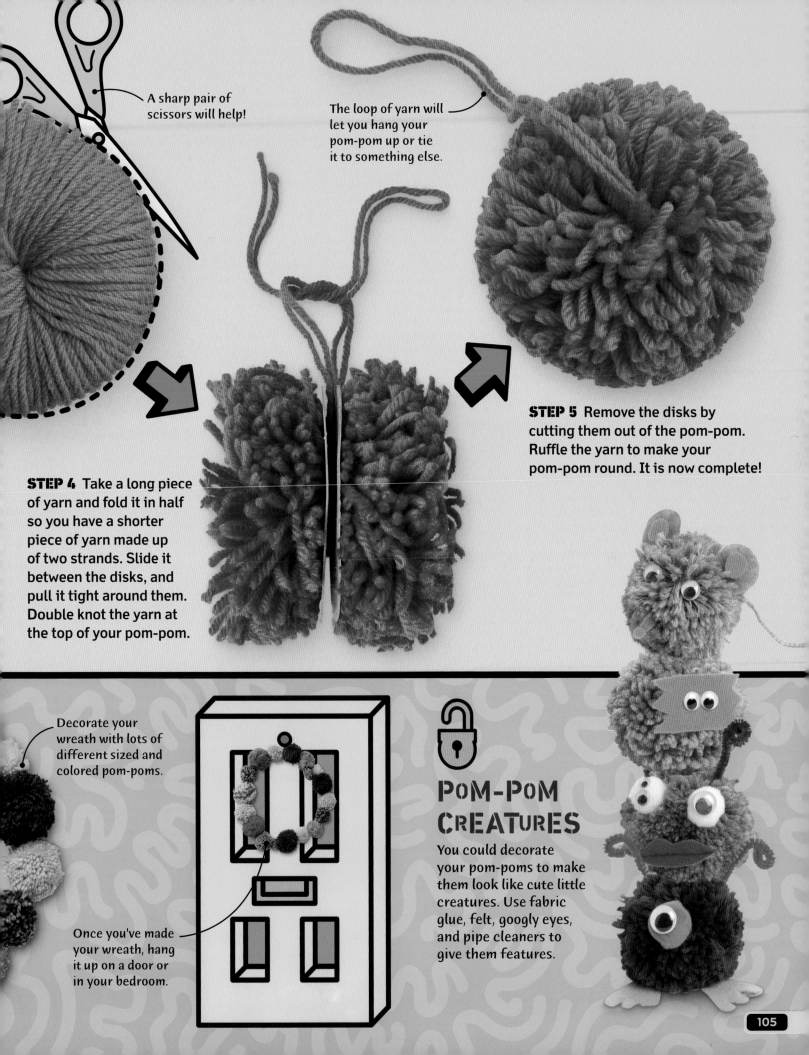

A sharp pair of scissors will help!

The loop of yarn will let you hang your pom-pom up or tie it to something else.

STEP 4 Take a long piece of yarn and fold it in half so you have a shorter piece of yarn made up of two strands. Slide it between the disks, and pull it tight around them. Double knot the yarn at the top of your pom-pom.

STEP 5 Remove the disks by cutting them out of the pom-pom. Ruffle the yarn to make your pom-pom round. It is now complete!

Decorate your wreath with lots of different sized and colored pom-poms.

Once you've made your wreath, hang it up on a door or in your bedroom.

POM-POM CREATURES

You could decorate your pom-poms to make them look like cute little creatures. Use fabric glue, felt, googly eyes, and pipe cleaners to give them features.

BECOME A
FASHION DESIGNER

Dream up out-of-this-world outfits, **sketch** your ideas on paper, then **make** them into reality.

167

Set the mood

! Designers often make a mood board to decide what look they're going for. You can make your own, either in a sketchbook or on a piece of poster board. Try adding bits of fabric, drawings, magazine clippings, stickers, and photos—whatever inspires you.

(168)

Get sketching

Once you've thought up a design, start sketching. Use pencil to draw the outfit's outline, then add color to make it pop. Will you go for bright tones or softer hues? Galactic patterns or down-to-earth designs?

(169)

Customize accessories

⚠ Give an old accessory, such as a bag, new life. Add paint, glitter, and pom-poms, or cut shapes out of fabric and stick them on with fabric glue. It's a double win—you'll practice your styling skills and get a new statement piece in the process. Fabulous!

Cut different shapes out of felt.

How to tie-dye

⚠ Create a cool new look by tie-dying a T-shirt! You'll need to buy fabric dyes and follow the instructions on the packet carefully. Wear gloves, an apron, and old clothes so that you don't stain anything. Make sure that any surfaces are also covered.

YOU WILL NEED:

- Rubber gloves
- Apron and old clothes
- Fabric dyes
- Buckets
- Salt
- White T-shirts
- Rubber bands
- Hot water

STEP 1 Put on your old clothes, apron, and gloves. Mix up the fabric dyes in the buckets according to the instructions on the packet. Add about 10 oz (275 g) of salt to the mixture to make the colors stronger.

ⓘ70 TIE-DYE T-SHIRTS

NOW TRY DIFFERENT PATTERNS!

TOP TIP
You can add several colors to your T-shirt by dipping each part in a different color, or by using fabric sprays on the different areas.

Rosettes

STEP 1 Bunch up different areas of the T-shirt, and tie rubber bands around each area.

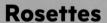

STEP 2 Push a finger into each rubber band to make a doughnut-like shape out of each area of the T-shirt.

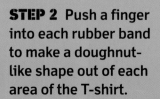

Swirl

STEP 1 Hold a fork in the center of the T-shirt with the prongs facing down. Twist the fork until most of the material is twisted.

STEP 2 Gather the material into a circular shape, and wrap four to six rubber bands around it.

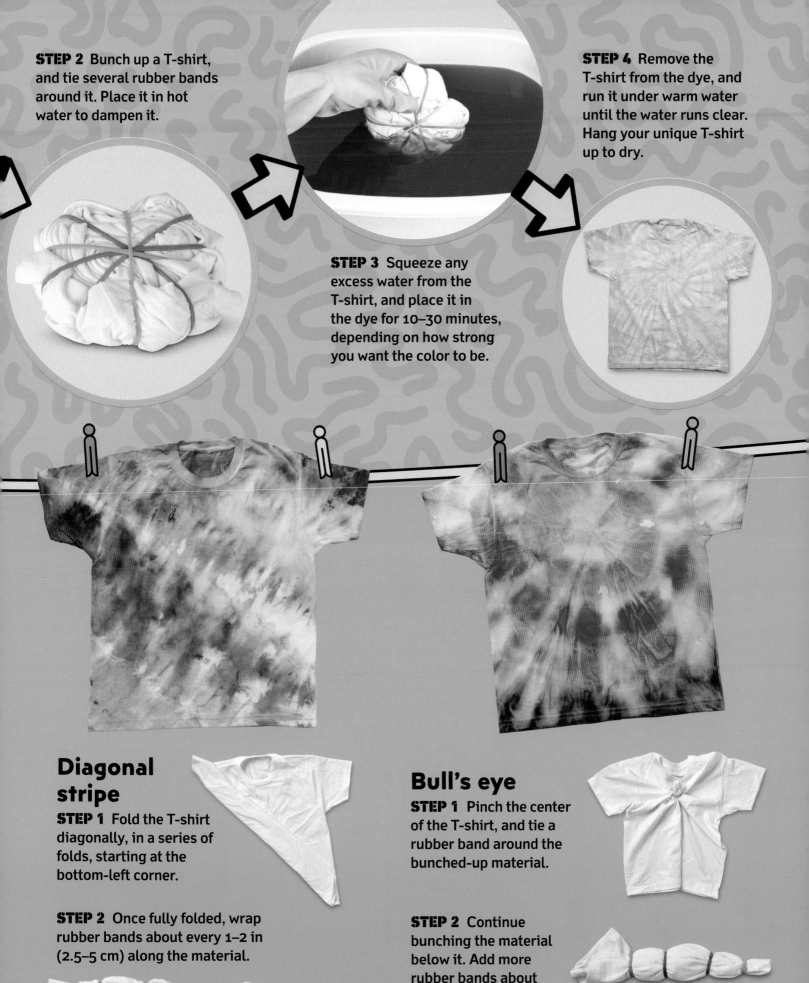

STEP 2 Bunch up a T-shirt, and tie several rubber bands around it. Place it in hot water to dampen it.

STEP 3 Squeeze any excess water from the T-shirt, and place it in the dye for 10–30 minutes, depending on how strong you want the color to be.

STEP 4 Remove the T-shirt from the dye, and run it under warm water until the water runs clear. Hang your unique T-shirt up to dry.

Diagonal stripe

STEP 1 Fold the T-shirt diagonally, in a series of folds, starting at the bottom-left corner.

STEP 2 Once fully folded, wrap rubber bands about every 1–2 in (2.5–5 cm) along the material.

Bull's eye

STEP 1 Pinch the center of the T-shirt, and tie a rubber band around the bunched-up material.

STEP 2 Continue bunching the material below it. Add more rubber bands about 1 in (2.5 cm) apart.

(171) MAKE A FLIP-BOOK

Turn your simple **drawings** into a fast-paced **animation** with the help of a **flip-book**. Quickly flick through the pages and be amazed as your images **come to life** before your very eyes!

STEP 1 As well as a pen or pencil, you will need either a sticky-note pad, a stack of paper clipped together, or a small notebook.

This will be the first part of your animation.

STEP 2 Draw an image on the last sheet of paper. Make sure it is close to the right side to make it visible when you flip through the book later.

The jets are firing up...

STEP 3 Draw the same image in the same spot on the second to last page, but make a small change. This will make the image look like it's moving when you flip the pages.

STEP 4 Keep drawing a slightly different image on each page to develop the story.

STEP 5 Keep going until all the pages are full. If you want, you can color in your drawings once you're happy with them.

The last image should be on the first page of the pad of paper.

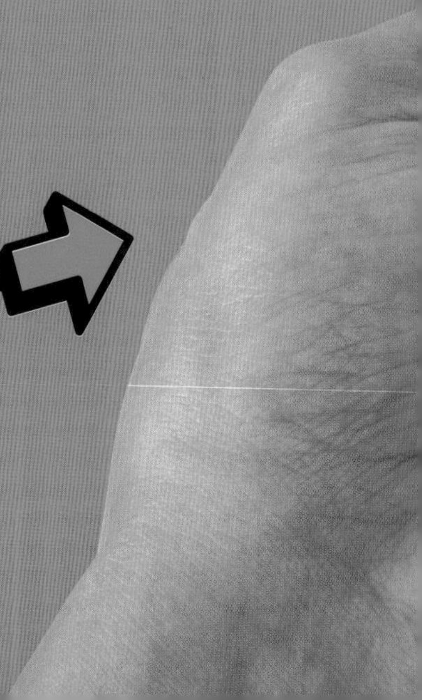

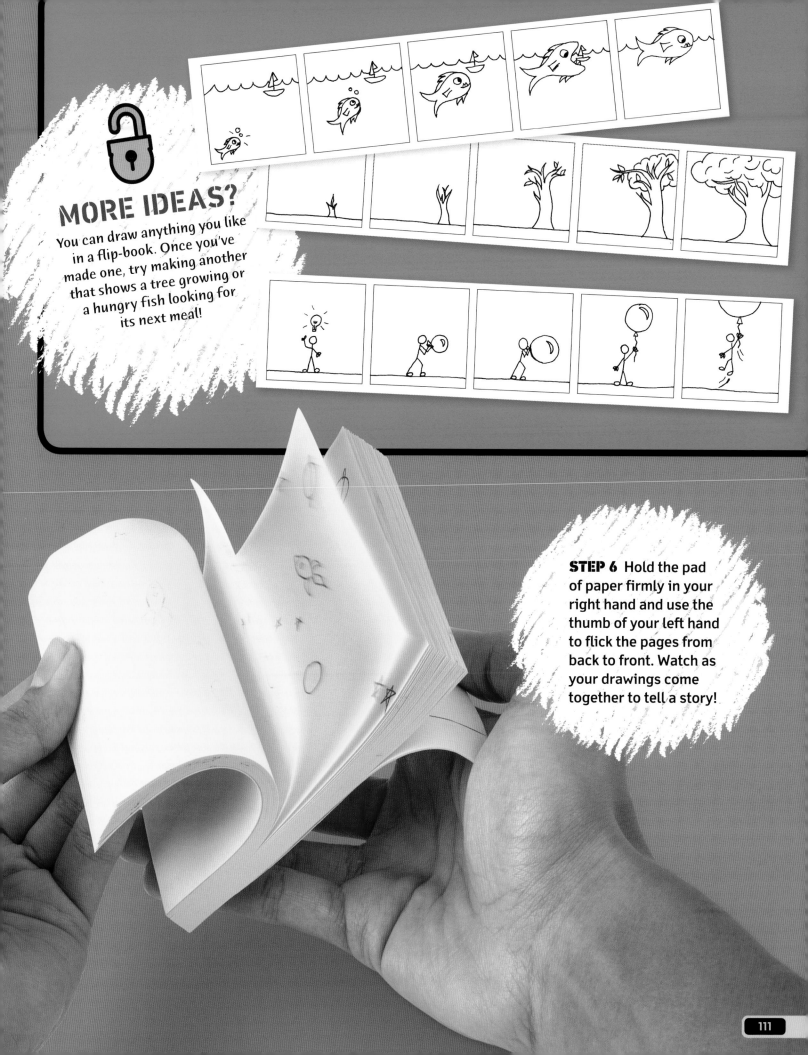

MORE IDEAS?

You can draw anything you like in a flip-book. Once you've made one, try making another that shows a tree growing or a hungry fish looking for its next meal!

STEP 6 Hold the pad of paper firmly in your right hand and use the thumb of your left hand to flick the pages from back to front. Watch as your drawings come together to tell a story!

PARTY GAMES

172 The tray game

STEP 1 Put 15 random objects on a tray, and cover them with a towel.

STEP 2 Remove the towel, and give the players 60 seconds to memorize as many objects as possible. When the minute is up, cover the objects again.

STEP 3 Players must now write down as many objects as they can remember. The winner is the player who remembers the most objects.

173
Laughing game

STEP 1 Players sit in a circle and take turns saying, "Ha, ho, and hee."

STEP 2 If someone starts to laugh out loud, they're out. The winner is the last player left that hasn't laughed. It's trickier than you think!

174
20 questions

STEP 1 You can play this game with two players or in a larger group. One player thinks of an object, and the others take turns asking them a "yes" or "no" question to try to figure out what it is.

STEP 2 If the object is not guessed before all 20 questions have been asked, the player answering the questions wins. This player then thinks of a new object. If the object is guessed correctly, swap players.

175
Wink murder

STEP 1 Players take turns being the detective. When the detective is chosen, they are sent out of the room. The remaining players then decide who is going to be the murderer.

STEP 2 The detective comes back into the room and stands in the middle of the other players, who are all sat in a circle.

STEP 3 The murderer's job is to wink at the other players, who "die" when they are winked at. When a player "dies," they must dramatically collapse to the floor. The murderer must avoid being caught by the detective. The detective has three guesses to uncover who the murderer is.

STEP 4 If the murderer "kills" everyone without the detective accusing them or if the detective guesses incorrectly three times, the murderer wins. If the detective discovers the murderer, they win.

176
Blind man's bluff

STEP 1 Find a big space and move everything out of the way. You will need a blindfold to cover one of the player's eyes.

STEP 2 The player wearing the blindfold stands in the middle and everyone else spreads out and begins walking around. Running is not allowed!

STEP 3 The blindfolded player must catch someone and identify them. If they are correct, the caught player is blindfolded. If they are wrong, they have to catch someone else and identify them correctly.

177

Bull's-eye

Use colored chalk to draw five different sized circles within one another. Each circle is worth a certain number of points. Players take turns scoring points by throwing a beanbag into the circles, aiming for the bull's-eye in the center.

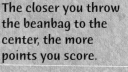

The closer you throw the beanbag to the center, the more points you score.

To make it harder, you could use balls that roll instead of beanbags.

5 4 3 2 1

SIDEWALK CHALK

Recess at school isn't complete without a stick of chalk. Try out these fun **sidewalk chalk** games with your friends, or show off your **artistic** flair with a chalk **drawing**.

! ALWAYS KEEP CHALK AWAY FROM YOUR EYES AND MOUTH. MAKE SURE YOU WASH YOUR HANDS AFTER HANDLING IT.

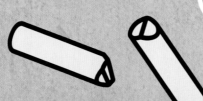

You must hop on one foot on single squares and land with two feet on double squares.

If you miss a square when you throw the ball, or step on a line, or lose your balance, you skip a turn.

1 2 3 4 5 6 7 8 9

(178) Hopscotch

The first player throws a ball into the first square and then hops through the course, skipping the square with the ball in it. The rest of the players repeat this same step. After all the players have completed the first square, they do the same with the second, third, fourth squares and so on. The winner is the first person to reach the end of the hopscotch.

Each player is given a ball as their marker.

The ball must stay within the square and not touch any of the lines.

STREET ARTIST

Once you've mastered a simple chalk image, move on to something bigger and better. Why not try drawing a huge city or a towering dinosaur?

(179) Giant pictures

Create giant outdoor masterpieces using colored chalk. Let your imagination run free and draw your favorite animal, a beautiful flower, or even a self-portrait. Try making them life-size so that they look real.

Be careful not to smudge the chalk while you're drawing.

PLAYGROUND GAMES

You don't need fancy equipment to have a great time in the **school playground** during **recess**. All of the games on these pages are for playing with a **group of friends**.

The strongest member of your team should go at the back.

181 Duck, duck, goose

One person walks around a circle of sitting players tapping each head and saying "duck." When they tap a head and say "goose," the goose gets up and chases them around the circle. They have to try to sit in the space left by the goose before they are caught!

You never know who will be the goose!

Walk around the circle in a clockwise direction.

180 Bulldog

Everyone lines up facing one person— the bulldog. The aim is to run past them without being touched. If the bulldog touches someone, that person becomes a bulldog, too. The remaining players then turn around and try to get past the bulldogs again. Continue playing until only one player is left—the champion!

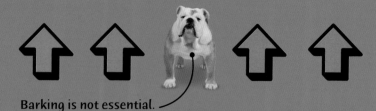

Barking is not essential.

182 Telephone

Sit in a line or a circle. One person whispers a sentence to the person next to them. They then have to whisper the same sentence to the person on the other side of them, and so on. The last person then says the sentence out loud. Has the message been passed on correctly?

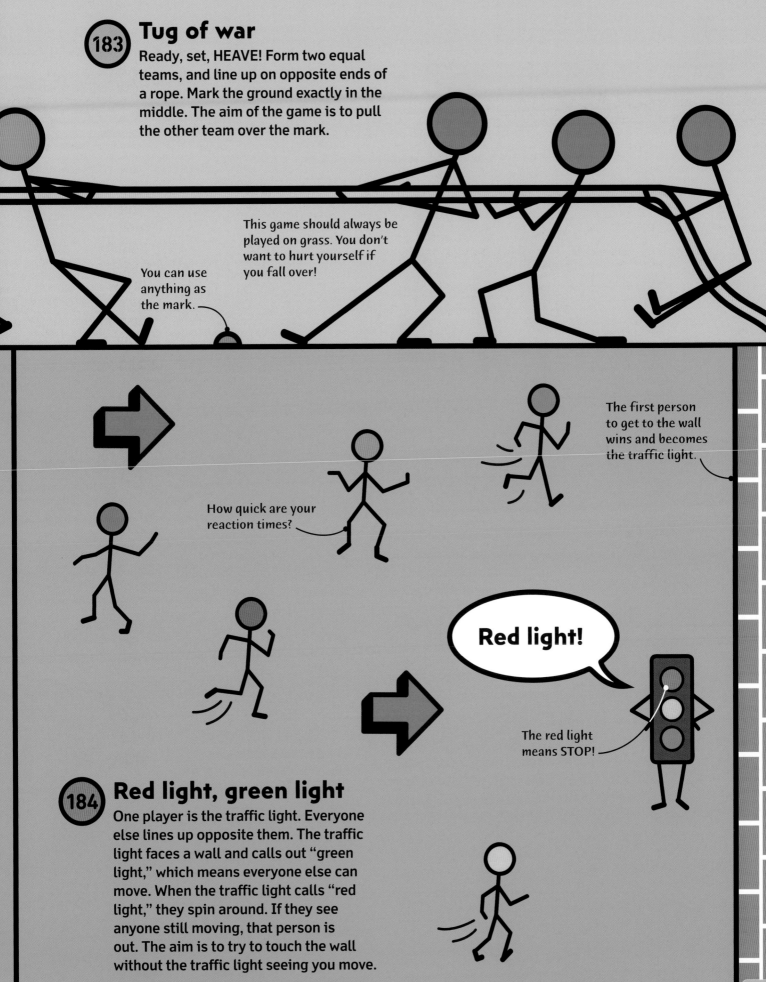

183 Tug of war

Ready, set, HEAVE! Form two equal teams, and line up on opposite ends of a rope. Mark the ground exactly in the middle. The aim of the game is to pull the other team over the mark.

This game should always be played on grass. You don't want to hurt yourself if you fall over!

You can use anything as the mark.

The first person to get to the wall wins and becomes the traffic light.

How quick are your reaction times?

Red light!

The red light means STOP!

184 Red light, green light

One player is the traffic light. Everyone else lines up opposite them. The traffic light faces a wall and calls out "green light," which means everyone else can move. When the traffic light calls "red light," they spin around. If they see anyone still moving, that person is out. The aim is to try to touch the wall without the traffic light seeing you move.

CARD GAME CRAZY

(185)

Chase the ace

3+ players

STEP 1 Give each player the same number of counters, such as buttons or pieces of popcorn or candy.

STEP 2 Choose a player to be the dealer. The dealer deals one card to each player, facedown. Players can peek at their own card, but should not show it to anyone else.

STEP 3 The goal is to get the highest card, a king. Aces are lowest, so you don't want to end up with an ace! Starting with the player to the dealer's left, each person decides to either keep their own card or to swap it for the card of the person to their left.

STEP 4 If at any point in the game you get a king, the highest card, turn it faceup. No one can swap with you—you're safe!

STEP 5 After each player, including the dealer, has had a chance to keep or swap their card, the round is over. Everyone turns their card faceup on the table. The person with the lowest card has to put one of their counters into the middle.

STEP 6 Keep playing, changing dealers every round, until everyone has lost all of their counters—except for one person: the winner!

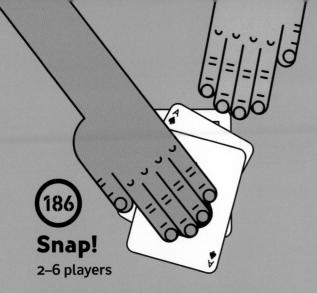

186 Snap!

2–6 players

STEP 1 Give each player an equal number of cards. They should keep their cards in a pile in front of them, facedown—no peeking! If there are any cards left in the deck, put them to one side.

STEP 2 Each player takes turns flipping over a card from their pile into the middle. The faster you go, the more fun the game is.

STEP 3 When two of the same card are flipped on top of each other, yell "Snap!" and slap the pile with your hand. The first person to do so gets to take all of the cards in the pile.

STEP 4 When you run out of cards, you're out. The winner is the person who gets all of the cards.

Go us!

187 Go fish

2–6 players

STEP 1 For 2 or 3 players, give each player seven cards. For 4 or more players, give each person five cards. Players can hold and look at their own cards. Fan out the rest of the deck facedown in the middle.

STEP 2 The player to the dealer's left begins by asking another player for a card. For example, they might ask, "Do you have any tens?" If that player *does* have tens, they have to hand them all over, and the asker goes again. If not, they reply, "Go fish!" and the asker picks up a card from the middle. If they get the card they asked for, their turn continues. If not, their turn ends, and the player to their left gets to go.

STEP 3 When a player has four of a kind, they can place the set face up on the table. The goal is to get the most sets. Keep playing until there are no cards left in the middle, then count up the number of sets each player has in order to see who has won.

188 Pig

5–13 players

STEP 1 Have players sit in a circle, and give each player four cards. Players can hold and look at their own cards, but not at anyone else's. Now get ready to move quickly— this game is a fast one.

STEP 2 Count down to start the game: "Three, two, one, go!" All at the same time, everyone passes one of their cards to the person on their left. Then again, and again, as fast as you can!

STEP 3 When someone has four of a kind, they push the tip of their nose up. Everyone else must copy them. The last person to do so is out. Deal the cards again and keep playing until only one person, the winner, is left.

Sardines in a team

STEP 1 This is a twist on Sardines (see below). There are a team of hiders and a team of seekers. You need to select an area that will be the jail.

STEP 2 Seekers close their eyes and count to 60 while the hiders hide in different places.

STEP 3 If a seeker finds a hider, the hider goes to jail. However, they can be freed from jail if a fellow hider comes out of hiding and manages to tag them without being seen.

STEP 4 If a hider is caught twice, they are out. The game ends when all of the hiders are in jail.

HIDE-AND-SEEK

189

Sardines

STEP 1 This game is best played in a whole house or backyard. One person hides while everyone shuts their eyes and counts to 60.

STEP 2 Time to search. When a person finds the hider, they join them in their hiding place, like sardines in a tin! This continues with each person who finds them.

STEP 3 The aim of the game is not to be the last person to find the hider.

STEP 4 The person who found the hider first becomes the hider next time.

191

Wave

STEP 1 One person is the seeker, and everyone else hides.

STEP 2 If the seeker finds someone, that hider then has to walk behind the seeker.

STEP 3 If the person who has been caught sees someone else hiding, they can wave at them. If the other hider waves back, the captured person can run off and hide again—as long as the seeker doesn't spot them doing it...

Have you ever played the **classic game** hide-and-seek? **Reinvent** it with these different takes on the original.

192

Shark in the dark

STEP 1 One player is selected as the shark. They hide in a dark room. The other players have to try to find them.

STEP 2 If the shark grabs your ankle before you spot them, you have to join the shark in their hiding place.

STEP 3 The game ends when someone finds the shark or the shark catches everyone else.

!
BE CAREFUL WHEN PLAYIN IN THE DARK MAKE SURE YOU CLEAR AWAY ANY OBJECTS THA YOU COULD TRIP OVER O BUMP INTO.

⑲③ TRAY CROKINOLE

Crokinole is a popular **tabletop** game that was invented in **Canada**. On these pages, you will learn how to make your own **crokinole board** and how to play!

YOU WILL NEED

- A large round tray (that you're allowed to draw on)
- A permanent marker
- Modeling clay
- 24 buttons (see step 3)

STEP 1 Turn your tray upside-down. In permanent marker, carefully draw the center circle, inner, middle, and outer rings, and the four zone lines.

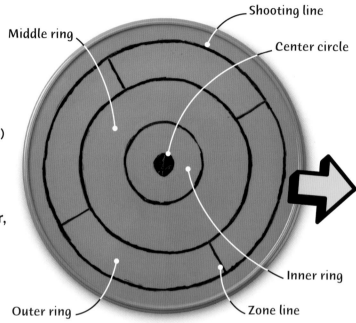

Shooting line
Middle ring
Center circle
Inner ring
Zone line
Outer ring

STEP 2 Position eight small pieces of modeling clay equally around the inner ring. These are called the bumpers.

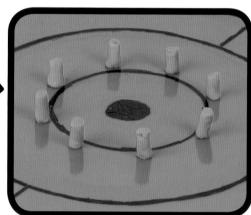

THE RULES

Game aim

Crokinole is usually played between two players. The aim of the game is to score the most points. Twenty points are given for pieces that land on the center circle. At the end of the game, 15 points are given for pieces in the inner ring, 10 points for the middle ring, and 5 points for the outer ring.

Each player takes control of opposite zones of the board.

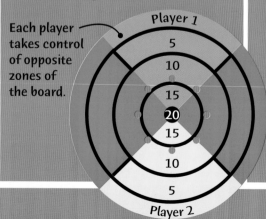

Player 1
5
10
15
20
15
10
5
Player 2

Starting

Flip a coin to decide who starts. Player one places one of their pieces on the shooting line of their zone. They must flick their piece onto the board using their index finger and thumb, aiming for the center circle. At the very least, their piece must end up in the inner ring. If it overshoots or undershoots the inner ring, the piece is taken off the board.

You can start anywhere along your shooting line.

Top score!

If player one's piece lands on the center circle, they are awarded the top score of 20 points. Note this down, and remove their piece from the board.

20
20
20

122

STEP 3 Collect two sets of 12 identically sized buttons to use as playing pieces. The two sets must not be the same color. Your crokinole board is now complete!

Practice flicking your pieces on the board.

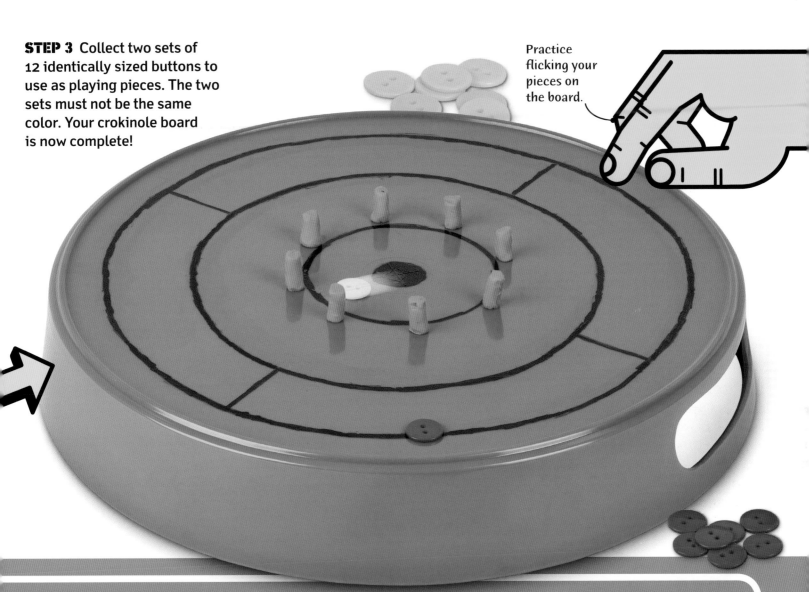

Second player

If player one's piece was taken off the board, player two can shoot at the center circle. However, if player one's piece is on the board in the inner ring, player two must attempt to flick it off the board or into a lower-scoring area with their own piece. At the same time, they should try to rebound their piece into a high-scoring area. Failure to hit player one's piece results in player two's piece being removed from the board.

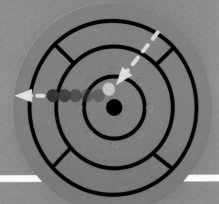

Crokinolin'

The game continues in this way—attempting to knock your opponent's pieces off the board with your pieces, and trying to land in the center circle—until both players have used all of their 12 pieces. If an opponent's pieces are on the board, you must hit at least one of them or your piece is removed. If at any point a player's piece lands on the center circle, it is removed from the board and that player is awarded 20 points.

End of the game

At the end of the game, add up the points. The pieces that remain on the board are awarded points depending on which ring they are in. The winner is the player with the highest score.

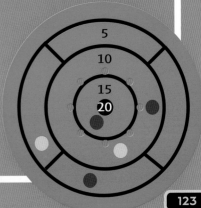

Table rugby

STEP 1 You need two people, a table, and a coin. The two players stand at opposite ends of the table. To start, one person places the coin on their side of the table. They then try to flick the coin over the table so that it hangs over the opposite side of the table. If they can't do it in three tries, the other player gets a turn.

You want your coin to end up here

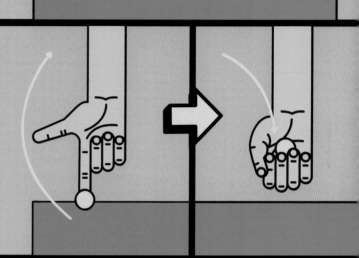

STEP 2 If a player completes step 1, they get one attempt to flick the coin up and then catch it in the same hand. Doing this is called a try, and it's worth five points. If the player doesn't manage it, it's the other person's turn (starting from step 1).

STEP 3 If a player manages step 2, they can try to get an extra two points by scoring a conversion. They must spin the coin on the table and then catch it between their thumbs mid-spin. If they don't catch it, the other person gets a turn (starting from step 1 again).

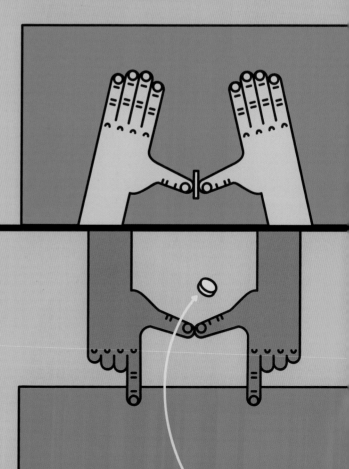

STEP 4 If a player achieves step 3, the other player makes goalposts with their thumbs and index fingers. The player with the coin holds it between their thumbs and tries to flick it above the other person's thumbs. If they get it over, they get the two conversion points. Then it's the other person's turn to start again. The winner is the player with the most points within a set time limit.

COIN GAMES

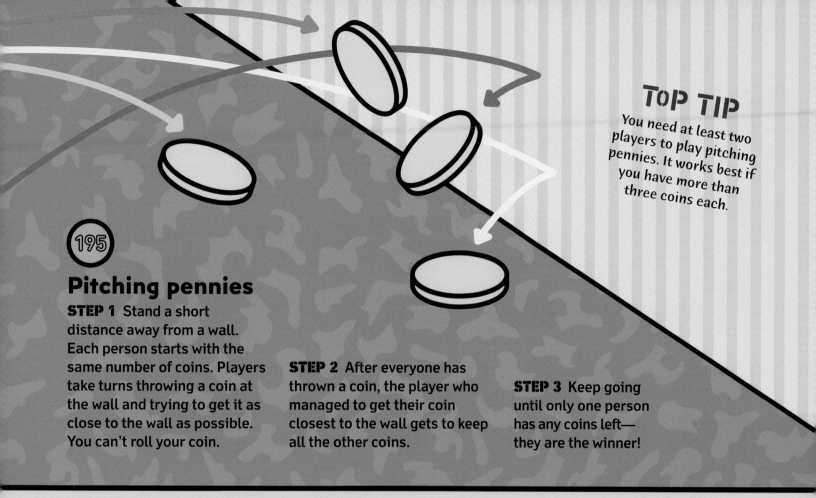

TOP TIP
You need at least two players to play pitching pennies. It works best if you have more than three coins each.

Pitching pennies

STEP 1 Stand a short distance away from a wall. Each person starts with the same number of coins. Players take turns throwing a coin at the wall and trying to get it as close to the wall as possible. You can't roll your coin.

STEP 2 After everyone has thrown a coin, the player who managed to get their coin closest to the wall gets to keep all the other coins.

STEP 3 Keep going until only one person has any coins left— they are the winner!

(196)

Spoof

STEP 1 Each player has three coins. Holding both hands behind their backs, everyone puts zero, one, two, or three coins into their right hand.

STEP 2 The players hold their closed right hands out in front of them. Everyone takes turns guessing how many coins there are in all the right hands put together. Each person must guess a different number.

STEP 3 Once everyone has chosen a number, players open their right hands. If anyone managed to guess the number of coins, they are out of the game. Then the players start again from step 1. The loser is the last person left at the end of the game.

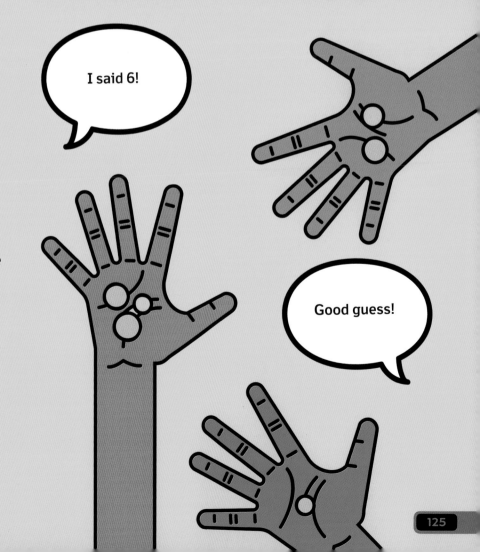

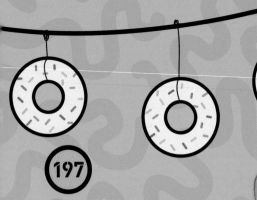

String eggs

With lots of string, some PVA glue, and a balloon, you can make a string egg. You could even make a few and string them together.

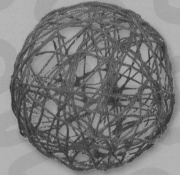

197

Donut game

Use string to hang donuts up on another string. Then try to eat them without using your hands. You can make this a race—who can finish their donut first?

STEP 1 Blow up a balloon, then cover it in glue. Loop string around and around the balloon.

STEP 2 Wait for the glue to dry, then pop the balloon. You'll be left with a string egg!

THINGS TO DO WITH...

201

String graffiti

Make patterns on a piece of paper with some string. Then use a toothbrush to flick paint onto the paper and the string. When the paint is dry, remove the string to reveal the patterns in the paint.

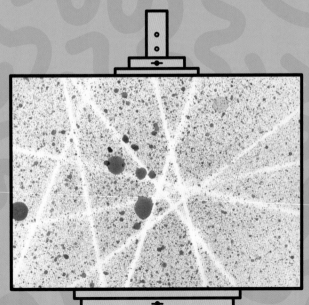

202

String sticks

You can use yarn or string to turn sticks into colorful decorations. Wrap the wool tightly around the stick. It looks best if you use a mix of colors.

203

Catch the spiders

Tie strings across a laundry basket and add some plastic spiders to make a fun multi-player game. Take turns seeing who can remove the spiders the fastest using tweezers or tongs.

200 Pick up an ice cube

With just a piece of string, you can pick up an ice cube! Wet the string, lay it over an ice cube, and add some salt. Wait a minute, then lift the string—the ice cube should be stuck to the end of the string.

The salt makes the ice melt and then refreeze around the string.

Make sure you add salt—the trick won't work without it.

199 String art

Loop colored or plain string into shapes, and then stick it down on paper. Now paint in between and over the shapes. The string will make parts of your artwork stick out and give it an unusual texture.

STRING!

204 Make a bracelet

Add differently colored yarn or strings together to make a friendship bracelet. It will look even better if you tie knots along it and add beads.

205 Limbo!

Tie your string between two objects. Then try to walk under it, but leaning backward as opposed to forward. Can you do it? What if you move the string even lower?

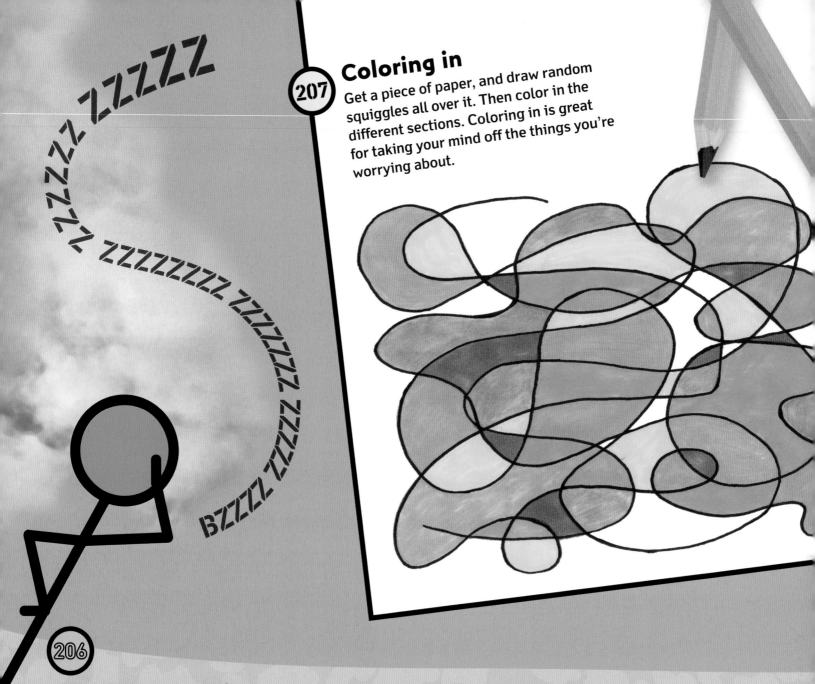

207 Coloring in

Get a piece of paper, and draw random squiggles all over it. Then color in the different sections. Coloring in is great for taking your mind off the things you're worrying about.

206 Breathing exercise

A good way to calm down is to focus on your breathing.

STEP 1 Place a finger on your closed lips, and breathe in through your nose.

STEP 2 As you breathe out through your mouth, make a buzzing bee noise. Feel it vibrate on your finger.

STEP 3 Place your hands over your ears, and breathe out while buzzing again. You will hear it inside your head!

CHILL OUT

Do you ever feel **stressed out**? The activities on these pages will help you **calm down**. You can do them whenever you need some **time to yourself**. Afterward you should feel like a weight has been lifted from your shoulders.

Cloud watching

(209) Lie down on a patch of soft grass and look up at the clouds. Can you see any recognizable shapes? Which cloud looks most like an animal?

I can see an aardvark.

TOP TIP
Take time to tune out distractions and focus on you.

Your hands should end up next to your feet.

Child's pose

(208) This is a very simple yoga pose you can do at home. Do it on a yoga mat or a piece of soft carpet.

STEP 1 Start on your hands and knees. Your hands should be beneath your shoulders.

STEP 2 Sit back on your heels, and stretch your hands out in front of you.

STEP 3 Lay your forehead on the mat, and bring your arms back by your sides. Shut your eyes, and relax...

(210) Crossing arms

This trick looks impressive, but it isn't difficult to do. It's all about timing. Start out jumping normally. Then, as the rope is coming down in front of you, cross your arms at the elbows. Jump through, and uncross your arms on the next downward swing. How many can you do in a row?

If you're tired of **jumping rope** the same old way, grab some friends and give these more **advanced jumping** activities a try.

JUMPING TRICKS AND GAMES

(211) Helicopter

Have one person stand in the middle and begin to spin a long jump rope in a circle along the ground. The other players must jump over it when it gets to them. Whoever the rope catches is out, until only one person, the winner, is left. Watch your feet!

TOP TIP
Don't worry about trying to jump really high. You only have to jump a little bit off the ground to clear the rope.

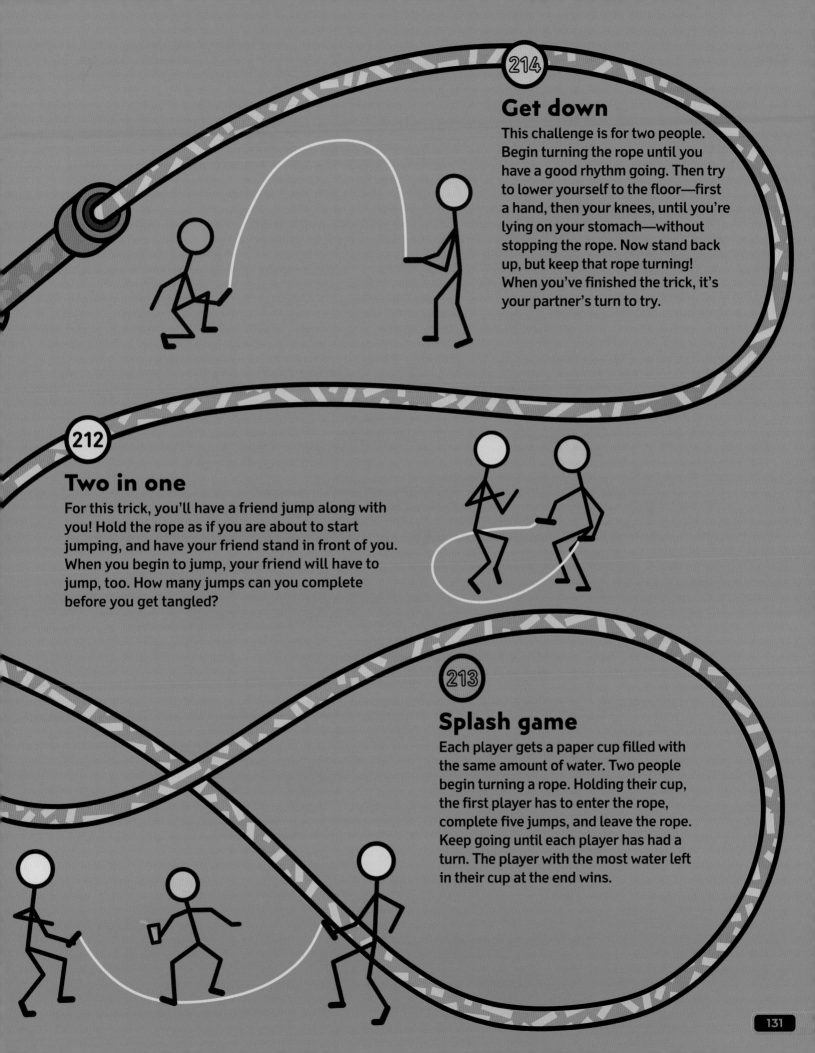

214

Get down

This challenge is for two people. Begin turning the rope until you have a good rhythm going. Then try to lower yourself to the floor—first a hand, then your knees, until you're lying on your stomach—without stopping the rope. Now stand back up, but keep that rope turning! When you've finished the trick, it's your partner's turn to try.

212

Two in one

For this trick, you'll have a friend jump along with you! Hold the rope as if you are about to start jumping, and have your friend stand in front of you. When you begin to jump, your friend will have to jump, too. How many jumps can you complete before you get tangled?

213

Splash game

Each player gets a paper cup filled with the same amount of water. Two people begin turning a rope. Holding their cup, the first player has to enter the rope, complete five jumps, and leave the rope. Keep going until each player has had a turn. The player with the most water left in their cup at the end wins.

YO-YO TRICKS

Yo-yos are terrific toys—they look cool, and they're quick to master. Follow the **instructions** on this page to take your first steps on the road to **yo-yo stardom.**

(215) The throwdown

STEP 1 To get started with any yo-yo trick, hold the yo-yo on its edge in the middle of your hand. The looped end of the string should be around your middle finger.

STEP 2 Turn your hand over, and let go of the yo-yo to send it down toward the floor.

STEP 3 When the yo-yo gets to the end of the string, pull up slightly on the string to make the yo-yo climb back up toward you.

TOP TIP

A good yo-yo will "sleep" (spin without moving up and down) at the end of its string.

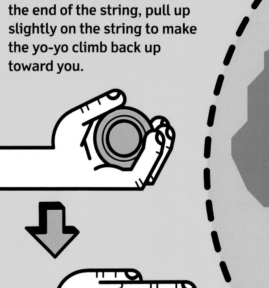

(216) Around the world

 Send the yo-yo straight out in front of you. When it gets to the end of the string, jerk your wrist up to send the yo-yo in a big circle. Pull the string to make the yo-yo return. Try not to hit yourself!

DID YOU KNOW?

Yo-yos were made in Ancient Greece more than 2,000 years ago!

(217) The forward pass

STEP 1 Start with your hand around your yo-yo, by your side.

STEP 2 Throw the yo-yo straight out in front of you. As it comes to the end of the string, pull on the string to bring the yo-yo back to you, then catch it in your hand.

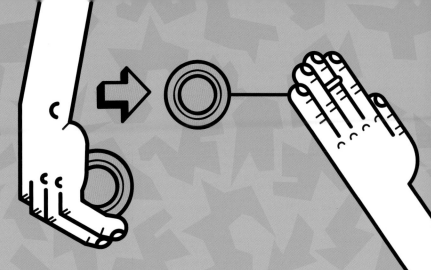

INVENT YOUR OWN TRICKS!

Once you've mastered these tricks, you can invent some of your own. Try changing hands, or looping the string around the fingers on your free hand in different ways while the yo-yo is spinning.

(218) Rock the baby

STEP 1 With your yo-yo sleeping, or spinning at the end of its string, loop the string over the first finger of your other hand.

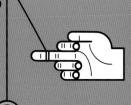

STEP 2 Bring your first hand under your second hand, with the yo-yo still spinning underneath them both.

STEP 3 Tuck the thumb of your second hand into the string, so that the string is over both first finger and thumb.

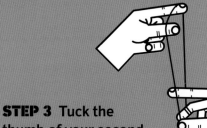

STEP 4 With your first hand, pinch the string near the yo-yo to make a triangle shape.

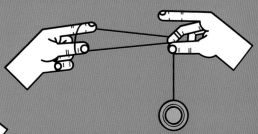

STEP 5 Take your first hand above your second to put the yo-yo inside of the triangle. Rock the yo-yo from side to side.

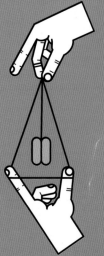

Make paper snowflakes

⚠ STEP 1 Cut a piece of paper into a circle, then fold it in half three times.

STEP 2 Cut out lots of different shapes along the edges of the folded paper.

STEP 3 Unfold the paper to discover a beautiful snowflake. Hang it from the ceiling to make it look like it is floating.

220 Snow sculptures

Building a snowman is fun, but can you imagine other shapes and creatures to make instead? For instance, you can build an animal, such as a bear cub or a dog—or an enormous T. rex!

Use snowballs to make your snow dog's ears and legs.

221 Snow angel

Lie on your back on a soft, snowy spot. Wave your arms and legs back and forth, then carefully stand up. Ta-da! You've made a snow angel.

(222) Make a snow globe

You can make your own magical wintry wonderland inside a jar using just a few simple pieces.

YOU WILL NEED

- Jar with lid
- Water
- Glitter
- Sticky tape
- Toy tree

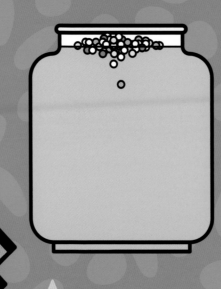

STEP 1 Nearly fill the jar with water, then add a sprinkling of glitter on top.

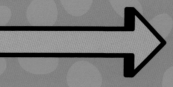

! TOP TIP

If the glitter is settling too fast, ask an adult to help you add a dollop of glycerine to the water.

STEP 2 Tape the toy tree to the inside of the lid. Tightly close the jar so the toy tree is sitting inside.

STEP 3 Flip the jar, and watch the glitter swirl!

FROZEN FUN

(223) Snowball lantern

! Children in Scandinavia make snowball lanterns at Christmas, and you can make them, too. Pile snowballs around a candle or flashlight to create a magical, glowing sculpture.

Main building

To make the main part of your castle you will need a big cardboard box—the bigger the better!

STEP 1 Keep the bottom of the box folded in, to make the castle's floor. Cut off the top flaps.

BUILD A CASTLE

⚠ Ever wanted to be **king** or **queen** of the **castle**? Here's how to build your own fortress from **cardboard**. Your enemies will tremble at the sight of it! You'll need lots of cardboard, and paint for decoration.

STEP 2 Cut up and down along the top of your box to make battlements. These are the gaps at the top of the castle's walls. Then cut a door shape as shown here, making sure you leave the sides of the doors attached to the box.

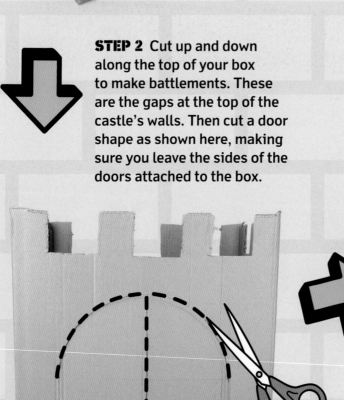

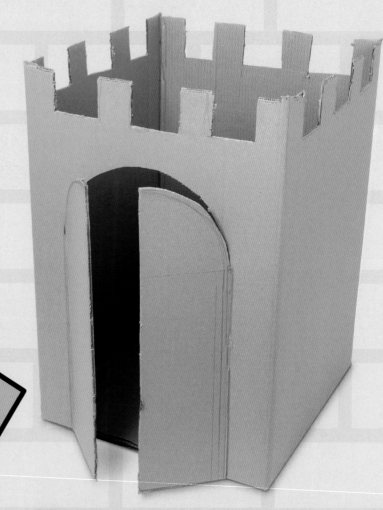

STEP 3 Push open the doors from the inside. Your main castle building is complete! You could add some windows to the door if you like.

Towering turrets

To make your castle more impressive, add some turrets.

STEP 1 Take a sheet of cardboard and roll it up. Stick strong tape down the edge of the card, to stop it from unrolling.

STEP 2 Get a second piece of cardboard and roll it into a cone shape. Use tape to hold it together, and trim the bottom to make it tidy. Place the cone on top of the tube. This is the roof of your turret.

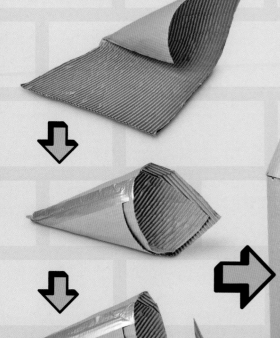

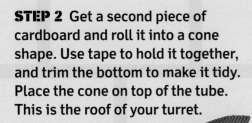

EXPERIMENT

Don't just follow these instructions! Why not customize your turrets? You could add battlements or windows, or stack them on boxes to make the towers even taller.

PUT IT TOGETHER...

A tall, thin cardboard box can make an impressive tower.

TOP TIP
Don't feel like you have to stick with your first castle layout—keep changing it until you think it's as good as it can be.

STEP 1 Design your castle layout. As well as your main building and turrets, try adding walls and boxes of different sizes. Get creative!

Make walls by cutting battlement shapes into long pieces of cardboard.

Smaller boxes are useful for helping other parts of the castle stand up.

A curved arch makes a grand entrance to a castle.

CASTLE DEFENSES
Our castle is just for fun, but many castle features were designed to keep the people inside safe from their enemies. The higher sections of the battlements were for archers to hide behind, so they could shoot arrows without being shot themselves.

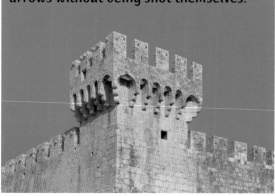

STEP 2 Add some final touches to your castle. You can make it as fancy as your imagination allows. Painting it will make it look even better!

You could add another piece of cardboard as a road into the castle.

You could paint the castle roofs a different color than the walls, to make them stand out.

Make roofs for square towers by folding a piece of card in half.

These flags are made from cardboard triangles stuck to wooden sticks.

Painting a brick effect on your walls will make your castle look more realistic.

...THEN PAINT!

139

BUBBLE FUN

With just some **water** and a dash of **liquid dish soap**, you can have hours of fun. Create different kinds of **bubbles** with items you find lying around your home.

225 Bubble wands

 Bend a wire coat hanger into a circular shape, and straighten out the hanger so it acts like a handle. Dip it in a mixture of liquid dish soap and water, and then swoosh it through the air!

226 Holdable bubbles

STEP 1 Mix together 4 tbsp (60 ml) of water with 2 tbsp (30 ml) of granulated sugar and 1 tbsp (15 ml) of liquid dish soap.

STEP 2 Put on a rubber glove, and gently blow a bubble onto your hand through a bubble wand. You should be able to hold it!

227 Cube and pyramid bubbles

STEP 1 Twist and bend pipe cleaners into pyramid and cube shapes.

STEP 2 Dip the pyramids and cubes in the bubble mixture, and see how the bubbles take on the different shapes of the pipe cleaners.

228 Bubble snake

⚠️ **STEP 1** Carefully cut off the bottom end of a plastic bottle.

STEP 2 Place a dishcloth over the end, and secure it with a rubber band.

STEP 3 Dip the cloth in bubble mixture, and blow through the other end to create a stream of bubbles.

229 Bubble painting

Add some food coloring to your bubble mixture to make your own modern art. Dip straws into the different colors, and gently blow the bubbles onto a canvas (or piece of paper). Don't suck the straws! Make sure some of them land on the paper whole—it makes a cool bubble outline.

BLINDFOLD GAMES

230

Blind animals

⚠️ **STEP 1** You'll need an adult for this game. Gather a large group of friends. Split into three or four smaller groups.

STEP 2 Tell each group they are a different type of animal—for example, horses, lions, and monkeys.

STEP 3 Make everyone except the adult put on blindfolds. The adult then moves everyone around so they are apart from their group.

STEP 4 You have to find the other members of your group by making the noise of your animal. The winning team is the one reunited first!

231 ## Key keeper

STEP 1 One person is blindfolded and sits on a chair with a bunch of keys underneath. The other players line up in a circle 10 ft (3 m) away.

STEP 2 Players try to grab the keys without the key keeper hearing and pointing at them.

STEP 3 When one player gets the keys without being heard, they become the key keeper.

(232) Piñata

⚠️ Make your own party piñata by filling a paper bag one-third of the way full of candy. Fill the rest with torn newspaper, and then staple it closed. Now decorate it with colored tissue paper. Make a small hole in the top of the bag, and hang it up with string. Take turns blindfolding each other and attempting to hit the piñata with a stick. If you're successful, you'll get treats! Alternatively you can ask an adult to buy you a piñata at a store.

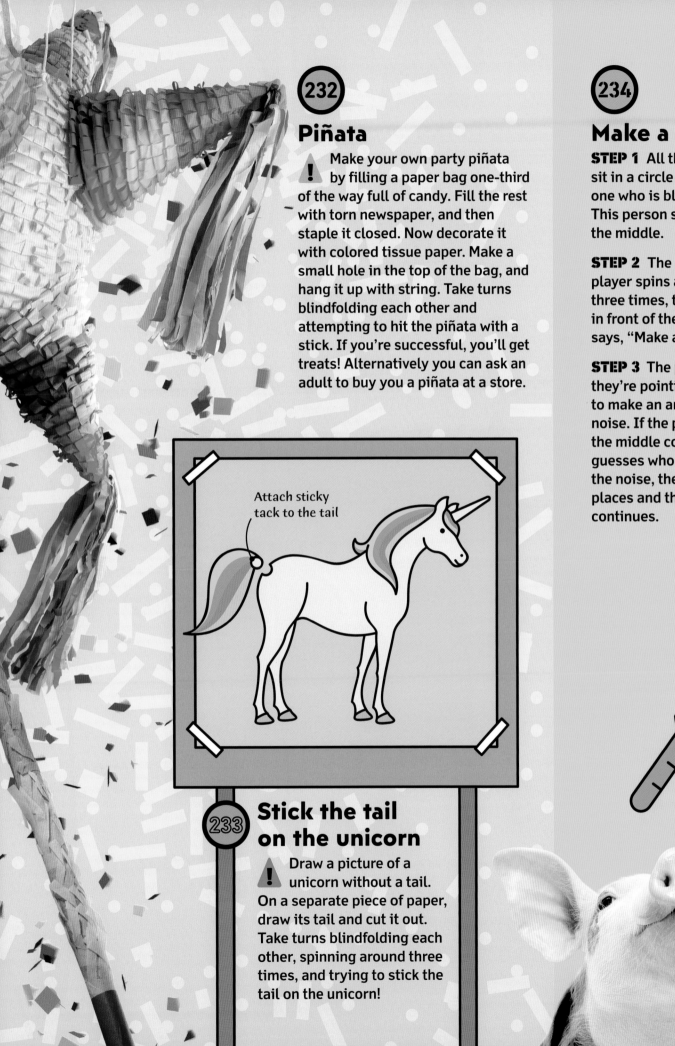

Attach sticky tack to the tail

(233) Stick the tail on the unicorn

⚠️ Draw a picture of a unicorn without a tail. On a separate piece of paper, draw its tail and cut it out. Take turns blindfolding each other, spinning around three times, and trying to stick the tail on the unicorn!

(234) Make a noise!

STEP 1 All the players sit in a circle except for one who is blindfolded. This person stands in the middle.

STEP 2 The blindfolded player spins around three times, then points in front of them and says, "Make a noise!"

STEP 3 The person they're pointing at has to make an animal noise. If the person in the middle correctly guesses who is making the noise, the two swap places and the game continues.

235 Escaped spider

Make a hole in a paper cup, turn it upside down, and write a message on it like this one. Anyone who sees it will think a scary spider has escaped from the cup.

SCARY SPIDER! Do not lift cup!

Eeeew!

SMACK!

236 Eat flies

Squash some raisins onto a clean flyswatter. Pick them off and eat them in front of your friends—they will think you're eating flies!

PRANK YOUR FRIENDS

Do you enjoy **tricking** people and making them **laugh**? It can be **funny** when things don't work the way you expect them to. Here are some **pranks** to play on your friends.

237 Toilet paper message

Write on a roll of toilet paper, so the next person to use it gets an unexpected message. What's the funniest message you can come up with?

It's behind you...

What's that smell?

144

238

Trick photography

Using funky camera angles, you can make it look like you're doing something strange, such as petting a giant dog. See if you can fool your friends.

239

Spilled drink

STEP 1 Make a pretend spilled drink using a paper cup, straw, and PVA glue on a plate. Wait for the glue to dry.

Add food coloring to the glue to make it look realistic.

STEP 2 Peel it off the plate, then leave your cup in a place where it will freak people out.

240

Secret shower

STEP 1 Use a thumbtack to poke tiny holes around the bottom of a plastic bottle. Then hold the bottle over a sink, fill it with water, and quickly screw on the lid.

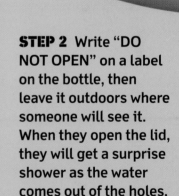

DO NOT OPEN

STEP 2 Write "DO NOT OPEN" on a label on the bottle, then leave it outdoors where someone will see it. When they open the lid, they will get a surprise shower as the water comes out of the holes.

It said not to open it!

STUMP YOUR SENSES

Put your senses to the test with these seemingly simple but truly **tricky challenges**. Using just your hands, your ears, your nose, and your brain, can you figure out **what's in the box**?

(241) **Touch test**

For your first challenge, you'll be using only your sense of touch to determine which mystery item is inside the box. Trust us, it's harder than it sounds!

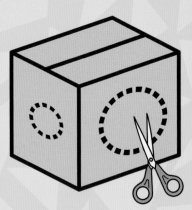

! **STEP 1** Grab a cardboard box of any size. Cut out a big hole on one side and a smaller hole at one end.

STEP 2 Have a friend put a mystery item inside the box. When it's all set, reach in and try to figure out what the object is just by feeling it. Your friend can watch the action through the hole in the side.

TOP TIP
Try wearing gloves for an even harder challenge.

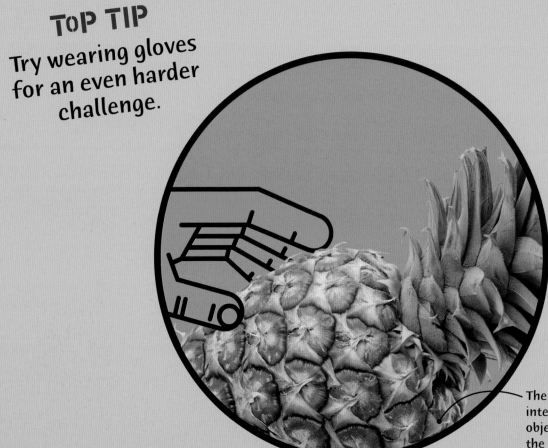

The more interesting the object feels, the better!

243 Listen up

Ask a friend to place an item in another box, one without holes, then seal it up. (Don't use an item that may break!) Can you guess what the item is by shaking the box and listening to its sound?

TOP TIP
Feeling how heavy or light the box is can also help you guess.

THUD!

RATTLE!
RATTLE!

242 What's that smell?

Use the box with a hole on two sides again. This time, ask a friend to put in something with a strong scent. Cover your eyes with a blindfold and take a big whiff. What's making that smell?!

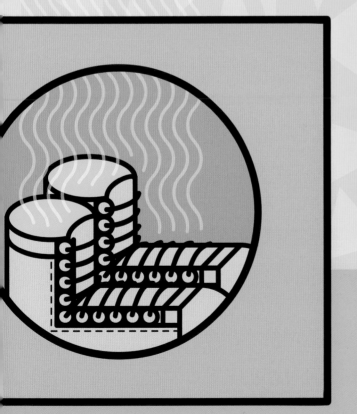

244 Take a guess...

Have your friend place a mystery object in the box with no holes. You have to guess what it is, but your friend can only answer your questions with a "yes" or a "no." Can you guess what's in the box in fewer than 20 questions?

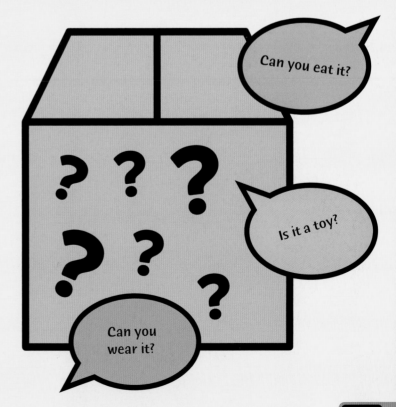

Can you eat it?

Is it a toy?

Can you wear it?

(245) MAKE A NEWSPAPER

Lots of people read newspapers, but have you tried **writing** one? Here are some ideas on what you could include. If this looks like too much to do by yourself, you could pull together a **team of friends** to help. Once you have your stories, lay them out, add some photos, and give it to people **to read**!

REPORTER SKILLS

A reporter is someone who writes stories for a newspaper. Here are some reporter skills you'll find useful as you put together your paper:

- Being curious: To find good stories, be curious—keep asking questions and searching for answers.

- Listening: Keep your ears open for new leads.

- Not giving up: It can take a long time to get a story right. Keep at it!

- Writing: You'll need to make subjects easy to understand for your readers.

Catchy headlines get people's attention.

DINNER THIEF ON THE LOOSE!

Find a story

You'll need plenty of stories to fill your newspaper. Head out and about to find some—is there anything interesting happening in your neighborhood you could write about? Exciting events make good stories, or you could interview family or friends. Try to keep your stories short.

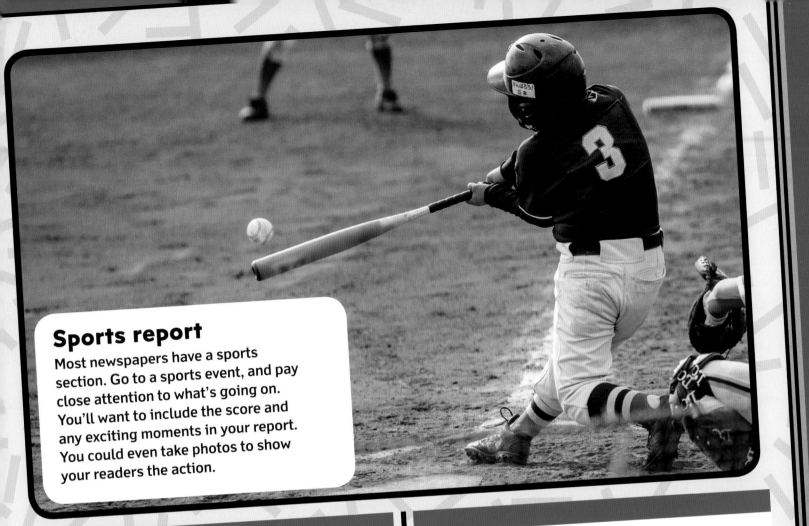

Sports report

Most newspapers have a sports section. Go to a sports event, and pay close attention to what's going on. You'll want to include the score and any exciting moments in your report. You could even take photos to show your readers the action.

Write a review

Reviews are a great way for your readers to decide if they want to see or read something. A review may describe a movie or book, then give an opinion on it without going into too much detail. If you haven't seen a movie recently, you could choose to review a TV show instead.

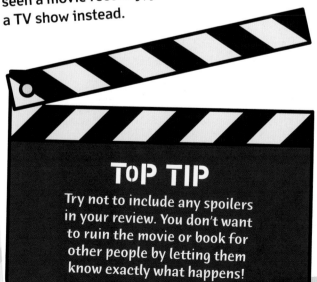

TOP TIP

Try not to include any spoilers in your review. You don't want to ruin the movie or book for other people by letting them know exactly what happens!

Give some advice

Think you're good at solving other people's problems? You can include an advice column in your paper. Advice columnists respond to questions sent in to them by readers—such as, "I think my friend is upset. What can I do to cheer them up?" The best answers are funny as well as helpful.

Dear Advice Amy,

(246) JUGGLING

Juggling combines great **coordination** with extreme **concentration**. When it works, it looks **awesome**. Here's how to do it with one, two, or even three balls.

One-ball juggle

STEP 1 Start off by juggling one ball at a time. Throw the ball from your right hand (if you're right-handed) to your left hand in a smooth arc. The top of the arc should be at about your eye level.

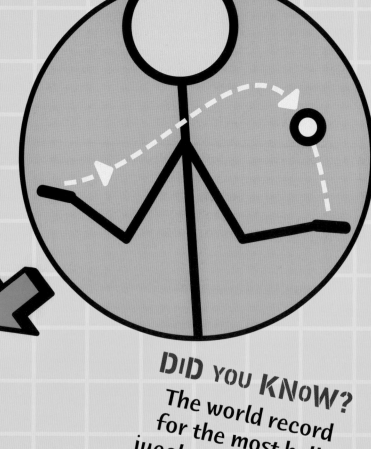

STEP 2 Now throw the ball back from your left hand to your right. Keep doing this until you can make a good arc from right to left and back again.

DID YOU KNOW? The world record for the most balls juggled at once is 11.

Two-ball juggle

Once you can juggle with one ball, add a second. As your first ball reaches the top of the arc, throw the second ball inside the arc of the first ball. Keep going until you can throw and catch both balls at the same time.

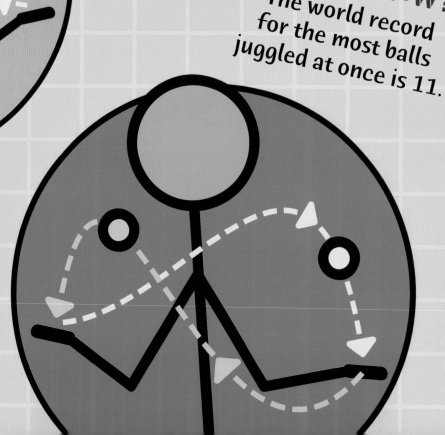

You can't look at all the balls at once, so pick a fixed point in the middle to focus on.

Three-ball juggle

STEP 1 Add a third ball. Hold two balls in your right hand, and one in your left.

STEP 2 Throw the first two balls as before. As the second ball reaches eye-level, throw the third ball inside the arc.

STEP 3 As the third ball reaches the top of its arc, throw the first ball and start the cycle again. Now comes the tricky part—keep going!

ADVANCED JUGGLING

Once you are able to juggle three balls, you can make things more difficult for yourself by juggling things that are different shapes, such as clubs—or see how many balls you can juggle at the same time.

247
Fire-breather

⚠️ Fix seven cups together to make your very own dragon. Poke small holes in the side of each cup with a pencil, then use paper fasteners to hold them together. Stick on googly eyes, draw the mouth and nose with a marker, and use white paper for the teeth. For a final flourish, add pipe cleaners to the nose.

248
Flower-grower

Fill your cup with soil and plant seeds. Add a sprinkle of water, and watch your flowers grow. Make sure there is a hole in the bottom so excess water can escape.

THINGS TO DO WITH...

252
Aim-tester

Write numbers on cups, then place them a distance away. If you toss a ball into a cup, add that many points to your score. Play against a friend!

50   20
10   5

253
Headband-decorator

⚠️ Cut triangles out of a cup's rim, glue pompoms to the top, and attach the cup to a headband to make a crown fit for royalty.

254
Sea-dweller

⚠️ With a bit of paint and a pair of scissors, you can turn a paper cup into an eight-legged pet! Curl up the paper tentacles using a pencil, and give your octopus eyes and a smile for extra fun.

250 Friend-caller

Poke a hole in the bottom of two cups. Get a long piece of string, and thread one end through each cup, finishing in a knot. When you pull the string taut and talk into one cup, your friend will hear you through the other.

SQUAWK!

249 Noise-maker

Tape the open ends of two cups together, with some dried beans or pieces of pasta inside. Add streamers for style. You've made your very own maraca!

251 Nose-changer

Draw the noses of animals on cups and gather your friends. Hold the cups in front of your faces and witness the transformation!

A PAPER CUP!

256 Cup-flipper

Place a cup on the edge of a table. Use one finger to push up against the cup's bottom to make it flip. Once you've got it, see how many you can land upside-down in a row, or in a minute.

The cup should flip all the way over in midair.

255 Pom-pom-popper

⚠ Cut off the bottom of a cup, and cut off the top of a balloon. Tie the end of the balloon in a knot, then wrap it around the cup. Add mini pom-poms to the cup, pull the knot, and—pop! Always aim it away from you and other people.

allergy
When certain foods or materials make a person sick

audience
Admiring crowd of people who watch a performance

blindfold
Material tied around someone's eyes to stop them from seeing

board game
Game that involves the moving of objects around a decorated board

bocce
Popular game that involves throwing heavy balls toward a small target ball

boundary
Line that usually shouldn't be crossed

card game
Game that involves playing with a set of rectangular cards that show symbols and numbers

character
Person who is in a story

checkers
Two-player game that involves moving round pieces across a black-and-white board

checkmate
Word said during a chess game when a player puts their opponent's king in a position where they can't escape

chess
Two-player game that involves moving different shaped pieces across a black-and-white board

compass
Object used for navigation that shows the directions North, East, South, and West

competition
Activity where people play against one another to win

compost
Decaying plants, food, and paper that is added to soil to help other plants grow

constellation
Pattern of stars or planets in the night sky

crokinole
Popular tabletop game played in Canada that involves flicking disks as close to the center of the board as possible

customer
Person who buys something from a store

defender
Player in a game who tries to stop other players from scoring or winning

dice
Small cubes showing a different number of dots on each side, ranging from 1 to 6

dominoes
Game that involves playing with small rectangular objects that each have a different number of dots on them

draw
When neither player wins or loses

escapology
Art of escaping from very tricky spots

experiment
Investigation to see how something works

genre
Type of story, such as adventure or mystery

golf
Game that involves hitting a ball into a hole using a special stick called a club

harvest
To pick fruits or vegetables so they can be eaten

illusion
Something that isn't as it seems

imagination
Using the brain to make things up

index finger
Finger next to the thumb

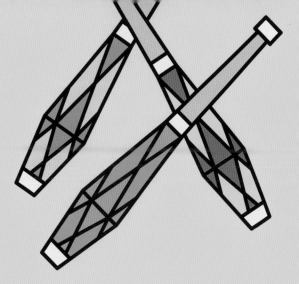

instructions
Information that tells you how to do something

juggling
Throwing multiple balls or objects in the air and catching them

key
Device that helps you understand what the different symbols on a map mean

laser
Type of light beam

lava
Red-hot melted rock

lyrics
Words in a song

mission
An important task that needs to be completed

multiplayer
More than one player

note
A high or low sound in a song

obstacle
Something that blocks the way

opponent
Person you're playing against in a game

origami
Art of folding paper into sculptures

paperweight
Object used to hold paper down

performance
Putting on a show to entertain people

permission
When an adult says you can do something

pom-pom
Woolen ball used for decoration

pool noodle
Long, bendy stick used in swimming pools to help you float

prank
Funny trick played on someone

recycling
Process of turning garbage into new objects

riddle
Question or statement phrased in a confusing way that has a clever or funny answer

rules
Information that explains how to play a game

score
Number of points each person or team wins in a game

specimen
Object that's been collected for study

strategy
Plan to win a game

Styrofoam
White, crumbly material, often found in packaging

supervision
When an adult watches over a game or activity

tag
Game that involves chasing or being chased

tie-dye Colorful pattern made by fabric dye

time capsule
Hollow object, such as a box or tin, that is filled with things to be opened in the future

INDEX